FINDING
Success
IN
BALANCE
MY JOURNEY TO THE
CHEERFUL MIND

APRYL ZARATE SCHLUETER

Finding Success in Balance: My Journey to The Cheerful Mind
Copyright ©2017 by Apryl Zarate Schlueter

Published by
The Cheerful Mind, Incorporated
Northbrook, IL 60062

ISBN: 978-0-9983203-0-4
eISBN: 978-0-9983203-1-1

Cover and Interior Design by GKS Creative

Publisher's Cataloging-In-Publication Data
(Prepared by The Donohue Group, Inc.)

  Names: Schlueter, Apryl Zarate.
  Title: Finding success in balance : my journey to the cheerful mind /
  Apryl Zarate Schlueter.
  Description: Northbrook, IL : The Cheerful Mind, Incorporated, [2017]
  Identifiers: ISBN 978-0-9983203-0-4 | ISBN 978-0-9983203-1-1 (ebook)
  Subjects: LCSH: Work-life balance. | Quality of life. | Stress management.
  | Happiness. | Success.
  Classification: LCC HD4904.25 .S38 2017 (print) | LCC HD4904.25
  (ebook) | DDC 306.3/61--dc23

For my super silly and cute babies . . .
Bubbagoo (Justin), Bubbaloo (Ryan),
and my puppy Leebs (Oliver)

CONTENTS

Introduction 1

Chapter 1. Apryl's Tips for a Healthy Work-Life Balance.....................11

Chapter 2. Family and Career: My Story...31

Chapter 3. Fun As a Value...55

Chapter 4. Health and Wellness 67

Chapter 5. Money Management Strategies 83

Chapter 6. Relationships 103

Chapter 7. Personal Development...119

Chapter 8. My Journey to The Cheerful Mind..143

    How The Cheerful Mind, Inc., Can Help You 146

Acknowledgments...155

Author Biography 157

INTRODUCTION

It's fitting that I finally felt compelled to write the first sentence of this book on a Saturday afternoon while simultaneously eating lunch, having a goofy conversation with my husband and children, sifting through a backlog of e-mails after a recent work trip, texting with a girlfriend about this afternoon's play date, and trying to clean up the house. This is my life. It's busy! It's crazy! There are so many things to do, and it frequently feels as if there's never enough time to get it all done. Once I conquer one challenge, more challenges arise. But you know what? I love it. Every single minute of it.

I don't know if I could say I loved it before now, though. I always used to feel overwhelmed, defeated, and exhausted from everything I had to do: raising a happy family, having a successful career and making good money, fitting in time for those I love, trying to find time to exercise and eat healthy, and making time for some plain old fun. I often went through the motions and spread myself too thin just to do it all, but despite the fact that I was accomplishing things, I didn't feel like I was executing well.

On the surface, I had a successful life, but more frequently than I desired, I still felt unhappy, unfulfilled, and stressed. Then, I made a huge life change because I was sick of sacrificing my happiness for all the "things" I had on my plate. I was sick of letting the never-ending checklist rule my life. I no longer wanted a "successful" life that someone else defined. It was time to take control and improve the quality of my life, while still getting it all done.

Fast forward to the present: my life has completely changed for the better. I can confidently say that I am happier now than I have ever been. I can have the fun I want in my life and although I am still extremely busy, I am more productive than ever before. My friends feel like they can't keep up with my whereabouts because I'm traveling so much, yet they are amazed I can still find time to give them love. I get to spend way more quality time with my family than I could before. I'm in the best physical shape of my life. I have a career I absolutely love. I have the confidence to go against the grain and try new things because I just don't have anything to lose anymore.

I'm not going to say it was an easy path, and the journey is definitely not over (nor will it ever be). I still experience hiccups here and there, but I am able to think more objectively and can efficiently resolve any problems that arise. The rewards I receive from my hard work, commitment, and dedication to improving my life are absolutely worth it. I write this book to share with you how I got here in the hope that I can represent what is possible—and to inspire others to do the same for themselves.

WHAT IS THE CHEERFUL MIND?

My name is Apryl. Yes, with a *y*. And because it's the first question 85 percent of people ask when they first meet me, yes—I was born in April. I am the Chief Energy! Officer and Certified Professional Coach for The Cheerful Mind, where I work with overcommitted individuals who are seeking a better balance in their lives; I coach clients in both private and group sessions and host workshops, retreats, and events to help them. When people work with me, they get the result of finding the time and energy to get it all done, while living an awesome, kick-ass life.

Using strategies and tools related to time-management, organization, and process improvement that I've successfully applied to my own life, my clients receive the benefit of increased productivity and more energy and happiness; they accomplish more and have more fun and an overall better, balanced quality of life. What is "better balance," you may ask? In the simplest terms, it's having fun while getting shit (and a lot of it!) done. (Pardon my language—the phrase just sounds so catchy, I couldn't resist. But if you're easily offended, remove the "sh." Just as effective!)

While most of my clients are working parents or entrepreneurial-minded like me, many other people can still benefit from the insights gained from my story in various ways: at different points in my life, I was that ambitious student, a single working professional, and a married working professional without kids. And you'll see as you read on that I've done many different things in my life that resonate with different types of people. In fact, if you've ever felt overcommitted, this book is absolutely for you.

So, let me tell you a little bit about my Chief Energy! Officer title. I've spent many years working for other companies and organizations, and we all know being a CEO is not the easiest job. I've always had high aspirations to move "up" the chain in my career, but I couldn't articulate what that really meant. Taking the leap to start my own business was never something I considered within my reach, but here I am. I can gladly say I'm my own "CEO"; however, it's not the usual CEO title. The "E" stands for Energy! (and please note the exclamation point is intentional). People who know me well say I'm like the Energizer bunny. I don't have much downtime—and when I do, it's planned. I have a cheerful attitude (hence, The Cheerful Mind), which comes from ten years as an athlete in cheerleading and over ten years of teaching and coaching it, as well. And I get A LOT done, which will be shared more in depth throughout the course of this book. When I realized what I was truly capable of, I decided to stop using my energy to complain and think negatively and start using it to help others fulfill *their* life goals, have fun, and get a ton done, too. Literally, I am my clients' personal cheerleader in helping them achieve the life they truly want.

HOW THE CHEERFUL MIND STARTED

The origin of my business is an interesting story. Prior to leaving my last job, I was speaking with my doctor about how to slow my mind down a bit. She recommended I see a meditation specialist and referred me to one she knew. Now, I had NEVER been the type who could sit still for long, and I definitely didn't think meditation was my thing. However, I have always been open-minded and willing to give anything a try. So, I met with this man who has practiced meditation and Buddhism for over twenty years. He runs a center in a northern suburb of Chicago. In the hour-long meeting, I told him my story, and he provided me with some powerful and interesting teachings. I was mesmerized by the thought of looking at my life through a different lens, although I wasn't quite sure yet how I could get there. We then practiced meditation. For the first five-minute trial, I giggled. A lot. It felt completely uncomfortable to me. But I completed it, and we tried again a couple more times. By my third try, I was able to calm myself and sit quietly for the full five minutes— an amazing accomplishment for me.

I left that initial appointment with so much energy—so much that I suddenly felt the need to make a "big statement" and embark on some sort of new journey. I sat in my car and started a Google search for domain names, thinking I would go big and share my journey with the world. For months, I had been asking myself what I ultimately wanted in life, and the answer was "to live happy, have fun, and be fulfilled." I immediately thought of the word "cheerful," since cheerleading was such a big part of my life, and "mind" because I knew I needed to adjust my mindset and the lens through which I had been looking for so many years. After a few iterations of domain name purchases and trying to grab corresponding social media handles, "The Cheerful Mind" was born.

Now, I had absolutely no idea what the hell I was going to do with it. Perhaps it would be a project by which I documented how I found my true happiness. Maybe someday I could make a business out of it, *if* I could come up with a decent concept. Over the next few months, I built the website. I highlighted my strengths based on my education and career background (attention to detail, problem solving, organization, time management, bringing order to chaos, streamlining processes, strategy), and my working style (I like big-picture thinking, but at the same time, I am very hands-on, and I love interacting and collaborating with people). I realized I could have so much fun helping people figure out ways to streamline their lives to achieve a better work-life balance and ultimately be happier as a result. Throughout numerous lunch conversations with friends, many asked me if I'd ever considered becoming a life coach. I didn't know much about coaching at the time, but I knew it would mean more school, and I wasn't mentally ready for that.

Several months later, I finally decided to look into life coaching certifications. I realized the work of a professional life coach aligns well with everything I said I wanted. Within days, I committed to a coaching certification program and was certified less than a year later.

During the training process, I quickly learned that I had been my first life-coaching client all this time: trying to find a better way to live life my way, do the things I truly wanted to do, and finally feel fulfilled. But because I had been so wrapped up in my own thoughts, I wasn't as effective at being my own coach. However, once I started personally experiencing the benefits of life coaching during my own certification process, I became a better decision maker and could take action more efficiently. Every time I conquered a challenge, I felt a great sense of satisfaction.

And I've been able to help some clients find resolutions very quickly; one client who needed much clarity on a career goal was able to find resolution in only five weeks!

My coaching style and programs are designed to do just that: teach people to set and accomplish their goals efficiently *and* have extra time and energy for more of the things they really want to do.

DECISION MAKING 101

People have to make decisions all day, every day. Some are relatively simple: What time do I need to wake up? Where am I going to eat lunch? My phone is ringing, should I answer? Some take a little more thought: Which of my friends do I want to call for a night out this Saturday? What kind of dress should I wear for a black-tie-optional wedding? Where should we go on our next family vacation? And some even MORE thought: Is this the person I want to spend the rest of my life with? How am I going to raise my child to be the best person he or she can be? What is the real purpose I am here on this earth to serve?

One of the fundamentals of conquering that overcommitted feeling is the ability to make better decisions. First, let me take a step back and say there's no right or wrong when it comes to making a decision. This may sound crazy to some, but it was a lesson that, once I learned to accept it (and trust me, I can be pretty stubborn), made my life much more easy to navigate. Every challenge presents an opportunity for you to decide which direction you want to take. That decision leads to another opportunity, and the cycle continues. There are no problems here, only solutions. Second, the only decisions you can control are your own. Everyone is going to make decisions around you, and those decisions will impact the decisions you make.

So, how do you make a "good" or "better" decision? Here's my advice:

Step 1: What does your gut tell you? Yes, the first thing I want you to tap into is your intuition. Which way is it leading you? Write that down.

Step 2: Logically, which decision makes the best sense for you? Step out of your own box for a minute, separate yourself from the outcome, and think about what makes the most sense. Write that down.

Step 3: Compare your answers in steps 1 and 2. Are they different? If so, ask yourself why? If they're the same, what does that tell you?

Step 4: Make a decision. Just go for it.

After you make that decision, observe how you feel. Are you happy? Relieved? Have mixed emotions? Are you sad? Angry? Pay attention to those emotions. They may be telling you something. I will explain more later about *why* this is so important, but just observe your feelings for now. I will say that if a decision you make is leaving you unhappy or unfulfilled, then it's time to make a new decision. And do your best not to dwell on what you believe is an "unsuccessful" decision. You absolutely need to make that decision before you can even see the one you consider "successful."

BALANCE AND THE WHEEL OF LIFE

The chapters in this book focus on the various areas of life, based on a coaching tool I use with clients called the "Wheel of Life" that identifies one's level of satisfaction in each of those areas. The topics include family, career, fun, health and wellness, money, relationships, spiritual awareness, and personal development. Each piece is important to the life equation, but they look different based on the individual. The "Wheel" concept was actually introduced to me some years ago during a lunch seminar at my work. It gave me greater perspective on where my life currently was, how I felt about it, and where I was yearning for greater satisfaction. That was probably the first time I knew I needed to make some changes in my life.

In this book, I share my story of how I found (or am still trying to find or improve) my definition of "success" in balancing all of these areas. Several important things to note: First, my path and decisions are a result of an unending series of trial-and-error experiments, and I didn't stop until I was happy with the result, readjusting along the way as needed. You don't need to be a genius or an expert at anything to find your own success, but you do have to work hard at it.

Second, my story will NOT be your story. I live my life in my own quirky way, and I don't expect anyone to understand it completely, but the point of this book is to inspire *you* to find your own way to own your quirks! So before I dive into it, thanks for coming along on this ride with me, and congratulations on taking the first step toward that awesome, kick-ass, high-quality life you've always desired.

one

APRYL'S TIPS FOR A HEALTHY WORK-LIFE BALANCE

Only recently did I realize I had been subconsciously working my whole adult life to find this "perfect" work-life balance. How could I have a successful career I love, one that would not take me away from all the other things I care about? Relationships with my family and friends, creating fun memories, staying healthy: these are among the many things I need in my life for ultimate fulfillment.

In hindsight, I now acknowledge that "perfect" may have been a bit of a stretch to achieve—let's just say I'm a "recovering perfectionist"—and boy, did it cause me a lot of stress trying to reach for that kind of lofty goal. But today, having a *healthy* balance is what I strive for, and I can say with confidence that I have been successfully working toward it. It's been a bit of a rocky road, but without those challenging times, I wouldn't have been able to learn from it and improve. Looking back on how far I've come, the payoff from all this hard work is completely worth it.

What are the feelings associated with having a healthy work-life balance? You feel at peace, you are happy, and stress levels are low. Conversely, being unbalanced leaves you feeling overwhelmed, like you're moving at a constant speed of a million miles per hour, unfulfilled, and with a certain level of dissatisfaction. Which sounds more desirable to you? In this chapter, I'm going to share with you some tips I've learned in my training and along my own journey that have allowed me to find success in balance—to feel more peaceful, reduce stress, and have the happiness I've always desired. In other words, I explain why I can now say with beaming energy and consistency that "life is amazingly good!"

TIP #1

Know that balance is not black and white—it's gray.
I recently had a conversation with a friend I hadn't been in contact with for a long while. He asked me how I was doing, to which I replied the usual, "[Sigh...] Great! So busy! So crazy!" and I rattled off the many things I was doing. I was still in my previous job the last time we'd connected, so I shared the progress of my new business venture. I also told him about writing a book about work-life balance, to which he responded, "Seems like that contradicts your real life!" I kindly disagreed and emphasized that my life is exactly how I want it to be.

It's really important to understand that the definition of

"balance" means different things to different people. Some people, like me, love to stay super busy. Others may think that is absolutely crazy and want to have as much free time on their calendars as possible. Some people actually like working longer hours, while others are out the door at 5:00 p.m. and don't even think about work until the next morning. Some people love working out daily, while others are fine with one day or two. Some want marriage and a big family, and some are completely happy being single. Whatever it may be, everyone has different priorities and desires, so to say that "balance" has a one-size-fits-all model is unrealistic. It's not always about having a little bit of everything and spending equal time on each area. It's about having the right amount of time for all the things *you* want in your life. And only *you* can determine what that is.

That said, drop all judgment and acknowledge that your own definition of balance will differ from others; what you consider a balanced life may not match anyone else's definition, and that is completely okay! It's more about achieving the feeling of balance than what you actually do to get you there. Don't let others define it for you. If it's quirky, but it feels good to you, then roll with it.

TIP #2
Self-awareness is the gateway to change.
Increasing self-awareness is probably the most important thing you can do to kick-start yourself toward achieving a healthier work-life balance. Being mindful of how you respond to any stimulus is absolutely essential in order

to make any meaningful changes in your life. If you're not paying attention, how can you decide to do anything different?

In any given situation, think about how your physical, mental, and emotional states are affected. For example, ask yourself the following types of questions:

- After a long workout, what physical pain do you feel in your muscles?
- How does sleeping only a few hours a night affect your ability to focus?
- What social situations do you thrive in, and which types of people do you like interacting with?
- How does the change in seasons affect your mood?
- What is the purpose of a task you are trying to complete?
- What types of scenarios really push your buttons and stress you out?

These are some sample questions that you can ask of yourself to become more self-aware. Once you know the answers to those questions, you can start to understand how and if those reactions serve you, and then decide whether or not it's time to make a change.

Sometimes it takes repeated reactions to the same situation before you even realize something needs to change (or maybe that you need more of the same). If you find yourself doing the same behavior over and over again, take note. If it's something that gives you great joy, what is preventing you from having more of it? If it's making you miserable, what will it take for you to change course?

One caution is that self-awareness is not the habit of forming a judgment about your responses; observations and judgments are two separate things. Observations are more informational and factual, while judgments are a filtered interpretation of an observation that may or may not actually be true, and they may skew your ability to make educated decisions. For instance:

Observation: *"I don't enjoy socializing in big group settings."*
Judgment: *"I have no friends because no one talks to me at parties."*

Observation: *"I like to leave work at 5:00 p.m. and not think about work again until the next morning."*
Judgment: *"I will probably never be successful because I don't bring work home."*

Know the difference between the two, and focus on staying as objective as possible as you are becoming more aware of yourself.

So how do you get started increasing your awareness and achieving that healthy work-life balance? Actually, you've already started by deciding to read this book, so congratulations! My advice is to continue reading and, as I share my story and journey, be mindful about the thoughts that come up about your own life. Have you experienced something similar? What did you do in those moments? What results did your actions yield? If you haven't experienced it, how might you have responded? Keep searching for your own answers and you'll be well on your way.

TIP #3:

Identify the values that drive your happiness.

One of the things you may notice while reading this book is the number of times I say the word "fun." It's among my top values and is so important to me that I have devoted an entire chapter to it. Accomplishment, communication, and respect are also important values. I love setting goals and meeting them. My relationships are optimal when open communication exists, and I place high priority on treating others as I would like to be treated. Once I took the time to understand the values that drive my happiness, I was able to make better decisions by aligning my actions with those values. Also, by understanding that my values may differ from others' helped shift my perspective and release a lot of stress. When I would experience conflict or rejection in an interaction, I used to take offense and sometimes harbor frustration toward that individual, not quite understanding their actions or opinions. Now, rather than being angry, I consider what is important to the other person and how it might differ from what is important to me. I am now more accepting of disagreement and sometimes even welcome and embrace it.

When you know your values, it is much easier to understand what is driving you to react a certain way in any given situation. When you are feeling happy, the values important to you are being honored. When you are faced with stress, one or more of your values is being challenged. Or it might mean that two or more of your values are in conflict with each other.

Have you identified your values? If not, a quick exercise could be to jot down a couple scenarios:

First, think of a time that made you happy. What was it about that particular event that brought you joy? Then, think of a time that caused you frustration. What specifically caused conflict in that moment? Your responses will give you some insight as to what values are important to you. (And if you still feel you need more guidance, get in touch with me—I would love to help you explore this further.)

TIP #4:

Know how to prioritize and plan.

Each week, we have seven days, or 168 hours, to get stuff done. How does the overcommitted individual seeking a better work-life balance make the most of that time? With a plan, of course! In order to streamline and maximize one's efficiency in life, a person constantly needs to identify the high-priority items on his or her to-do list, and then implement a timeline and plan to execute those items. Some tasks may only require a few minutes, while others may involve days, months, or maybe even years of tasks and subtasks before they are complete. While it is each individual's prerogative for exactly how long and how detailed to make their plan, highly productive individuals have a system, such as a calendar or an advanced, highly detailed to-do list, they use to track their progress toward their goals and ensure they are completed appropriately.

Why is it so important to prioritize? For overcommitted individuals, the to-do list never ends. If you spend most of your time executing tasks that are not important, you may be getting some things done, but you will likely lack the feeling of fulfillment. While we all have tasks to do on a regular basis in order to live (laundry, cleaning the house, shopping for groceries, paying bills, etc.), we must also balance them with tasks that align with our values and sense of purpose. And when we do this, we can feel more excited and invigorated about life.

Quite often, there appears to be a lack of time to complete multiple important tasks. In some cases, perhaps it will be necessary to place more focus on the highest priorities. But in other cases, there may be pockets of opportunity where time can be repurposed toward another task, as long as the main priorities can still be addressed. One way to assess the situation is to look at your schedule and locate those "gaps of opportunity." Are there similar tasks you can cluster together and resolve more efficiently? For example, if you need to make a handful of phone calls, can you schedule those calls in a consolidated window of time? Or could you run outside errands in an order that minimizes your driving time?

Ask yourself if there are areas of your life in which you spend *excess* time that you could sacrifice to achieve another goal. For example, if you want to find more time to work out, are you willing to stop staying at work late so that you can spend some time at the gym? One of my clients was interested in pursuing a new project in alignment with his passions, but felt he didn't have the time to execute it. We evaluated where he was directing his energy and how much time he spent in these areas. Once he was able to see the true amount of time he was devoting to personal care, work, family, and all of his other commitments, he was able to see that he indeed had "gaps of time opportunity." It then became a decision of whether or not he really wanted to repurpose some of that time toward his pet project.

Are you spending a lot of time complaining about how much work you have to do and how much is on your plate? If the answer is yes, are you really aware of how *much* time you spend complaining? Could this time be repurposed into actually getting your work done? I laugh at these questions because this was my biggest time waster and productivity killer. I'm not saying to never vent or complain at all because sometimes it helps to unload the stress you have. *But,* be aware of how long you spend in that space. Is it worth that time that you could be otherwise getting other things done? Just some food for thought.

One last thought on planning and prioritizing: I suspect some of you may be struggling with having to commit to *any* plan. Maybe you want to have that wiggle room to deal with opportunities that come up at the last minute. Maybe you don't want to commit to something that could potentially be derailed. You know what? That's perfectly fine! If that's important to you, go with it. But just know you're *planning* to not have a plan. And while that's all fine and dandy, how does it rank on your priority list?

TIP #5:

Embrace flexibility.

After all that talk about planning, it's just as important to acknowledge that change is inevitable. You can be the type of person who can plan things down to the minute (ask anyone who went to my wedding about the thirteen-page spreadsheet I created, outlining the responsibilities of every single person in my wedding party from 6:00 a.m. to midnight that day), and perhaps everything will go great without a hitch. However, it can just as likely result in completely unexpected outcomes. For those who are super-planners like me, it is essential to know how to be flexible because when plans go awry, you may experience a lot of unnecessary stress.

I've learned this lesson the hard way, multiple times. For instance, I had once orchestrated a vacation where I arranged in advance separate plans with eleven different people over four and a half days, and when a couple of the meetings didn't execute as I had anticipated, putting forth all that effort prior to the trip and not being able to see those plans come to fruition was frustrating. Furthermore, I spent a lot of time during the vacation trying to make adjustments, and I wasted a lot of time that I could have otherwise been having fun. After that trip, I vowed to "wing it" a little more and, while I may still have some plans while on vacation, the only thing I really commit to now is making sure I have fun, and that seems to work wonderfully.

While we are on the topic of vacations—which by the way sound really fun right now—there are SO many examples where lack of flexibility causes stress. How much do you love those delayed flights? Or better yet, how about those flights that get canceled as you're already strapped into your seat and ready to go? What if you had a three-week cruise setting sail the following morning? Imagine how stress and anger would serve you in those moments. Trust me, they don't. And while stress is not ever 100 percent avoidable, how you manage that stress quickly and get through it is key. So, after you throw your internal mini-tantrum and get over the initial shock of your world being suddenly turned upside down, start looking at your options. In this case:

- Are there other flights that will get you there in time?
- Can you drive?
- Is there a train you can take?
- Is it worth canceling the trip or rescheduling?
- Should you start looking at alternative ways to get to the next port of call?
- Where is your luggage, and how will you ensure it gets to where it needs to be?

There are opportunities to resolve the issue, but as I mentioned earlier, the longer you linger in your anger, the less efficient you will be in getting anything done.

So in a nutshell, plans are always subject to change, so be flexible. If your master plan hits a roadblock, don't waste your time stewing in your own anger; quit complaining and take action toward a solution—you'll be much more productive that way. Say, "Bring it on, change! I *will* conquer you!" You'll likely manage to figure out a way to get things back on track and make things work, and then have an amazing and potentially funny story to tell.

TIP #6:

Be open minded about trying new things.

If you have a FOMO (or "fear of missing out") attitude, this might come easy to you. And that's great because you don't have many adjustments to make to execute this tip. It's easy to give anything a shot because, really, what do you have to lose? If you try it and you like it, you can do it again. If you realize after the fact that it's not your thing, at least you have a good story to add to the memory bank.

For those anti-FOMO folks who struggle with wanting to try new things, I have a question for you: What's stopping you from doing something new or differently? Okay, I understand if it's just something that doesn't seem exciting or interesting to you, but that's not what I'm talking about here. What I'm asking is this: If you want to make a legitimate change in your life toward something that would make you happier and more fulfilled, what is stopping you from trying something new that might lead you one step closer to what you *really* want?

One of the biggest roadblocks people may encounter is their fear of change. Having to adapt to any sort of scenario different from the norm can bring up a number of mixed feelings, mostly in the form of stress. Considering the pain that the thought of change can bring, it's completely understandable why people may not want to step outside their own boxes. Many find comfort in maintaining status quo and in some cases, this is fine; however, when your heart desires more, living with the same patterns isn't going to address those aspirations. You must either choose to set aside those dreams or finally face that fear and take steps to change.

Some people might believe they have limitations that prevent them from achieving what they want (not enough time, not enough money, etc.). Why should that stop you from even trying? What are some tactics you can explore to get that money, time, or whatever else it is that limits you? For instance, if money is an issue, perhaps you can consider requesting financial support, especially if your investment will bear a greater return in the long run. If time is what you are lacking, look for those "gaps of opportunity" and make this change a priority. Look for the opportunities; don't just jump to conclusions.

Others just flat out don't like to fail. Understandable, but failure is what allows you to grow. How can you know what you like if you don't know enough about what you *don't* like? Don't immediately consider failure a bad thing; sometimes people have to fail in order to open their eyes to the opportunities that come afterward. And if you have tried multiple strategies that have failed, don't lose faith in the success of other strategies. Just because the track record isn't ideal doesn't mean you won't ever find success.

Finally, some are concerned about how others may judge their actions. Keep in mind that these other people are *not* you. Whether or not they approve of your life decisions is irrelevant. Only *you* know what's best for you. If they truly care about you, they will support you no matter what.

With all that said, I will admit I have been guilty of all of the above at certain times. I have had a lot of fear. I made assumptions. I cared way too much about what other people thought. Once I realized I could let all of that go, the sky was the limit. I do trip up occasionally and revert to my old ways, but I stay aware and immediately switch out of the negative, self-defeating mode of thought when I catch myself. And I haven't been happier. Note: I NEVER thought I would write a book. And here you are, reading my book. Just saying.

TIP #7:

Know your boundaries.

Of all of my tips, this one is probably the most impactful, yet the hardest one for overcommitted people to execute. Recognizing my own boundaries was one of the toughest lessons I needed to learn, and perhaps others in the overcommitment camp can relate. In some cases, I choose to take on all challenges that arise without seeking help from others because I don't want to burden anyone else with my issues. Everyone is busy and dealing with their own to-do list. Other times, knowing how overwhelming life can be, I want to help people who seem to be drowning in their tasks, and because I care about them, I take it upon myself to help them toward a less stressful state. Unfortunately, that can also leave me with a lot of responsibility on my plate, less time, and more stress.

There are two things to realize about setting boundaries. First, you must draw the line and say no to outside requests from time to time. You're not superman or superwoman, and you can't do it all. You may wish you could, but you can't. Actually, wait—think about how much pressure comes with being a superhero: People *depend* on you to save them, but if you spend all your time saving others, who will come to your rescue when you need it? Perhaps you need to learn how to be just a little bit selfish about what *you* need, especially if no one else is going to give you those things. You need to allocate your energy toward doing those things for yourself.

If you're a giving person, I know this is easier said than done. I struggle with this often, and I continually ask myself what it truly means when I say no to others in order to make time to take care of myself. Does it mean I'm self-centered? Absolutely not. It just means I am treating myself as I would any family member or close friend, and there's absolutely nothing wrong with that. So here's a thought: Remember when we talked about values? When someone asks something of you and it doesn't align with your values, that request is something you should say no to. I encourage you to try it.

The second thing to know about boundaries is there are people out there who *can* and *want* to help you. Utilize your support system. This can be your friends, family, or anyone you come in contact with on a regular basis. And if you have the means, paid services exist to assist with the many things you have on your plate. If you are a parent, getting help with your children, whether paid or free, is a great way to free up some time for yourself to do other chores, or to relax and have a night out, or maybe even to sleep in.

Imagine how that would affect the quality of the time you spend with your children when you are with them. Maybe you're a professional who works long hours or travels for work frequently; you might not want to spend your entire weekend going to the grocery store, but still want the fridge full of options when you are home. Perhaps you consider a grocery or food delivery service to save you that trip to the store. There are services out there that are meant to save you the time that you don't have. Take advantage of them.

It's time to exercise the power of *no* in order to start saying *yes* to you. Outsource the things that drain you, so that you can make time for the things you really want to do. It's not the easiest task, but I promise when you finally take the leap, it's an amazing feeling.

TIP #8:

Get really good at multitasking.

This is the tip where some of my work-life balance expertise shines through, as I am the queen of multitasking. Let me first start this tip by saying that I am not encouraging anything dangerous like texting and driving. And I'm not saying that you should multitask anything that requires serious focus. As I mentioned earlier, think about the Wheel of Life and how you can multitask in the different areas it covers (as a refresher—career, family, money, personal development, spirituality, relationships, health and wellness, and fun). For example, how can you have *fun* and fulfillment in your *career*? How can you foster good *relationships* while at the same time addressing your *health and wellness*? How can your own *personal development* bring you more *money*?

As you continue this book, I'll show you how I've found a way to make working out fun and gain so many friendships while doing it. I have a career that aligns with my passions and allows me to spend more time with my family and friends and take a ton more vacations. I've worked hard on my personal development and as a result, I am the healthiest I've ever been. I found a way to create more wealth, even in the absence of a 9-to-5 job.

When you can align your actions to enhance multiple areas of your life simultaneously, you can also save precious time. And as you know, there's never enough time in the world of the overcommitted. The more aware you are of how the tasks you execute strengthen your connection to your values, the closer you are to mastering your work-life balance.

TIP #9:

Slow down.

Sometimes it's easy to forget to breathe when you have so many things going on. But we need to breathe in order to live. Whenever you start to feel unhealthy tension in your muscles, get up and walk around. Take a few deep breaths. If meditation is your thing, do it. If working out helps you blow off some steam, perhaps go for a run. If you like to belt out tunes, go for a drive or hop in the shower and sing your heart out! Whatever it is that you need to do to release that tension, go for it, because that tension is indicating you're probably moving too fast.

Overcommitted people work at a fast pace and understandably so, considering there's never enough time in the day to get every single thing done. But just remember that life is short, and on occasion, you need to stop and appreciate all the gifts you have been given. If you don't, what's the point?

I once had a chat with a client whose intuition led her to feel that *I* was overwhelmed due to the rushed energy I brought to our conversation. I was absolutely not aware this was happening, but as soon as she pointed that out, I felt sick to my stomach because it was true: I was trying to get some other work done, while scarfing down my breakfast at the same time, moments before we got on the call. I hadn't made any space to take a breather beforehand. I can't imagine how effective I could have been trying to help someone else who felt overcommitted find the room to breathe when I wasn't "walking the talk." From that point on, I decided that it was time to slow down. As a result, I'm feeling a lot more peaceful, while still getting the same amount (if not more) done.

If you are a planner, I would suggest plugging enough buffer time into your schedule that you're not rushing from one thing to another without time to breathe. For example, I literally type "Transport" into my calendar whenever I'm driving to/from appointments. It prevents me from trying to overload my schedule and helps me find a way to say no without guilt. Most importantly, it brings me one step closer to my ideal work-life balance.

TIP #10:
Make a commitment to balance and don't give up.

Committing to something new can be difficult for people who already feel overcommitted, but if you're interested in conquering the work-life balance challenge, it's necessary because it takes persistence and hard work to get there. Changing how you live your life into one that's less overwhelming and more fulfilling doesn't happen overnight. You're not always going to find the right solutions to your problems the first time, or the second time, or maybe even the third time. There's a lot of trial and error involved in making good progress. But with the proper perseverance, you will get there.

Sometimes your life will just be hectic, and you need to prepare extra hard for those occasions. But if you start thinking ahead and know you'll need some rest after a stressful time, block the time you need to recuperate.

Take a moment to imagine a goal you set and accomplished. Think about all the small victories you celebrated as you worked toward achieving it. Think about all the things that didn't work along the way that may have caused frustration. Think about the feeling you had when you finally achieved the goal. What did that accomplishment inspire you to do next? Now think about work-life balance:

- How much do you want it?
- What are you willing to do to get there?
- How do you think you'll feel as you make progress?
- What might it inspire you to do next, once you get to where you want to be?

***

So there are my tips to have that great balance in life you've always wanted. You've probably noticed that some of the tips may appear to cancel each other out: be a good planner, but be flexible; try new things, but set boundaries; multitask, but slow down. If you know what the extremes are and can avoid them, you're much more likely to seek the middle ground. And that middle ground, my friend, is the sweet spot. I'll see you when you get there.

two

FAMILY AND CAREER: MY STORY

To gain a real understanding of how I arrived at my current stage in life—the Chief Energy! Officer of The Cheerful Mind—it's important to go back to my roots. Family is the foundation of everyone's lives. Out of the womb, the parental connection is the first thing children experience. All family interactions from that point forward influence a child's growth and development into the independent adult he or she eventually becomes: the rules by which parents (or guardians) raise him, the exposure to and importance of education, the bonding of siblings, and many other factors all play a role in shaping the individual.

In this chapter, I share the story of my family upbringing, my career path, and my road to being a parent. I share the main drivers of my success in these areas, the decisions I made, and how I have worked relentlessly to have the career and family I've always wanted. What you'll notice is how my values influenced my path, how my awareness guided my decisions, and that trying new things finally led me to my cheerful mind. Keep in mind how my story relates to your own experiences and life, and know that you can find your cheerful mind, too.

FAMILY VALUES

My parents were born and raised in a northern province of the Philippines. My father was the eighth of nine children, and my mother the youngest of nine. They were both raised in an environment where money was extremely hard to come by, and their lifestyle was worlds away from American standards. They both were extremely intelligent and driven, desiring a better life for themselves.

By means of his older sister, my dad was given the opportunity to come to America in 1977, and he joined the United States Air Force Reserves to further his education beyond his bachelor's degree in biological sciences, which eventually helped him secure a job as a biochemist in a Chicago hospital. My mother was quite the entrepreneur in her twenties: she had a degree in banking and finance and worked as a successful sales consultant for beauty products in the Philippines. My parents carried on a long-distance relationship, marrying in 1978. I was born two years later, and my mother and I flew across the world to join my dad in starting a brand-new American life.

Because my parents knew poverty, they desired a life of

success, and money was extremely important to them. They worked very hard so I would never have to experience what they did as children. My parents teamed up and worked multiple jobs, frequently working opposing shifts to make ends meet. Usually one parent was working while the other one was with me, or both parents worked while another relative helped take care of me. They saved every penny and only spent what they deemed was necessary. (Clipping and sorting coupons was definitely a childhood memory of mine.) Due to the high cost of raising children, they contemplated only having one child, but being children from larger families, they thankfully graced me with a baby brother five years later.

Career status is extremely important in the Philippines. Parents have a strong influence on their children's career paths, and professions are usually displayed on the outside of the family home for the public to see. Needless to say, this value carried over from the Philippines, and it was important to my parents that I worked toward securing a successful career, which to them meant one that provided great financial stability. In order to achieve a successful career, I needed to have a strong education. So as many Filipino parents do, my parents "strongly encouraged" me to seek a career as a doctor, lawyer, or engineer—and they did so very early on. I wanted to make my parents proud, so I kept those career paths in mind as I progressed through school.

GROWING UP

The biggest responsibility my brother and I had growing up was to work extremely hard—with the highest priority being on our education. We were raised with the "money doesn't grow on trees" mentality, and our success was defined by the results of our hard work in school. This success was extremely important to me, but it also carried some internal pressure and stress; I only missed class if I was bedridden or contagious, and almost always had perfect attendance marks. I usually cried when I had a grade lower than a *B*. Because education was the main focus, my parents did not allow me to have a paying job during my teen years. They also implemented financial incentives in exchange for high marks. They focused on making the money, and I focused on getting good grades.

I felt as if I were being raised in the culture where my parents grew up, and that discipline often conflicted with the American culture surrounding us. Sometimes I was resentful as a teen because I felt that I had little freedom in comparison to my friends. I always had an insanely early curfew, and whenever I misbehaved, they took the most beloved thing away from me—my telephone—for weeks at a time. I often felt they were unreasonably strict, and I definitely rebelled on occasion, especially when the reason they said "no" didn't appear rational.

Even though there was a strong emphasis on career and financial success in my family, we also strived to achieve balance. To make sure we were well rounded, my parents frequently took us on road trips all across the country; we went camping every year and visited the Philippines several times. We were raised Catholic and attended church on Sundays. We enjoyed relationships with friends and family by attending numerous parties where the adults could socialize and catch up while the kids ran around and played.

Still, my parents worked long hours and they were not always available, and even when they were, they were often tired from long work days. My parents supported my involvement in my extracurricular activities, such as cheerleading and choir, but they couldn't go to every single football or basketball game or every concert. Our family rarely had the opportunity to sit at the dinner table together because one parent generally worked in the evenings. I understood why this was necessary, but I did miss my parents a lot and wished I had more opportunities to spend quality time with them at home.

BECOMING AN ENGINEER

By my junior year in high school, I had numerous interests that I juggled simultaneously. Looking back, I see my tendency toward overcommitment began there. I loved both theater and choir and actively participated in my high school's musicals, plays, and vocal jazz and choir programs. I was also an athlete: a cheerleader, an ice skater, and a black belt in Tae Kwon Do. In addition, I took piano lessons for over ten years. I was taking mostly honors classes, enjoying math and science classes the most, but I also enjoyed a newswriting class for the school newspaper. In fact, an old yearbook says I intended to pursue a career in journalism.

I rarely slept, staying up until at least 1:00 a.m. every night, making sure my homework was complete (and correct) for the next day. I remember lugging all of my textbooks in my backpack around with me at school; I only put them in my locker if my homework was complete for the evening. I was a pretty intense student.

Knowing I had to choose a college major, and acknowledging the subliminal messages my parents had given me about becoming a doctor, lawyer, or engineer, I talked myself out of the fun idea of pursuing a major in music—*It won't pay much money, and I'm not a good enough singer anyway*—and followed my geek passion for physics and mathematics. The summer before my senior year in high school, I was admitted to a summer program at Northwestern University, which gave me a preview of college life for six weeks by living on campus and taking engineering courses. I chose courses in the mechanical and electrical disciplines, as well as exercise science. I fell in love with digital circuits, which eventually solidified my early decision application to Northwestern the following fall with a major in electrical engineering.

Once admitted to Northwestern, I knew I couldn't attend college without an activity on the side, so I tried out for the co-ed cheerleading team and made the squad as a freshman. I had a rocky start to college though. Coming from a strict upbringing, without much freedom growing up, I started having fun and socializing like crazy during my first quarter in college. And cheerleading was a demanding commitment during football season: sometimes up to twenty hours a week of workouts and games. My grades weren't so great, and it was the first time I felt failure. Big time. So I spent the remaining three and a half years focusing on cheerleading and school, trying to get my GPA back up to a respectable level by the time I graduated. I knew if I didn't get my grades up, I could not live with the thought that I'd wasted my parents' money and disappointed them.

TIME TO GET A J-O-B

During my senior year, I was at a loss about where I wanted to work. I had a part-time job at an engineering firm, but I wasn't interested in continuing full-time work there. I did not want to leave my family; it was extremely important to keep that relationship intact. I interviewed for a number of local engineering positions and recall how introverted and quiet the culture was. In one interview, I was introduced to one of the lead engineers as he worked diligently on some prototype at his desk. He turned to me, shook my hand in silence, and literally turned back to his work without saying a word. This was the first time I felt that I might be *miserable* in any engineering job. I knew that I was generally more outgoing than my engineer classmates, but this *really* started to concern me.

I started to reevaluate my career path: Had I made a mistake? Did I just waste four years of my life studying electrical engineering, only to throw it away? No way, I couldn't do it. My parents would be so disappointed in me. And I would have wasted so much money by pursuing a major with no relevance to my future. And yes, while engineering teaches some valuable problem-solving skills and techniques, I felt obligated to solve only engineering problems.

I started to doubt myself. I continued the full-time job search by widening my scope to IT consulting—an area where many of my friends were securing jobs. In talking with friends and corporate recruiters, I observed a more collaborative spirit and team environment that would better fit my personality. After a few months, I secured a job as a consultant doing data warehousing and reporting and had a blast traveling the world and working with some well-known companies and organizations. I immersed myself in this lifestyle for about two years. My parents were proud of my success and the money I was earning.

A SHIFT IN PRIORITIES

Although the travel and my compensation were awesome, my level of job satisfaction began to shift. I was assigned to a project in Australia and England for a few weeks, and my outbound flight was scheduled a couple days before my brother's high school graduation. Because my family is so valuable to me, I was not interested in missing that event. When I asked my boss if I could fly out a few days later, he responded: "You need to choose your family or your career."

Upon hearing this, I was devastated. How dare he ask me to prioritize between the two most important aspects of my life? Nevertheless, I resentfully (and how could you be resentful about a free trip to Australia?) took the assignment, and life went on at home without me.

I quickly realized this phase of my career was coming to an end. I loved my family too much and didn't want to be in a career that would take me away from them. What would happen when I had kids? Would I have to choose between my career and having children?

I started to give up on my hopes of continuing down the IT/engineering path and looked for a more predictable career. I recalled how in college I'd spent a summer teaching cheerleading to high school students and, during my two years as a tech consultant, I continued to teach occasional weekend clinics at local park districts when I was home. I found much joy working with the kids, and the puzzle started coming together. I pondered how I could make a career out of my love for math and science, teaching, and kids...

BECOMING MRS. SCHLUETER

I resigned from my consulting job after getting into a teaching certification program back at Northwestern. My biggest concern with this career switch was that further education would require a potential gap in employment and pay. I was a homeowner at that point and could not afford to be unemployed. So I sought a one-year, evenings-only alternative certification program that allowed teachers-in-training to conduct their student teaching requirement during a summer quarter and be hired as a full-time teacher the following fall. This agreement was tied to working in the city's public schools, which was fine with me. I knew the inner-city kids could use some great teachers, and I wanted to be a mentor to them. I also knew that working and being in school simultaneously was going to be quite rigorous, but I felt that I could manage just fine.

I completed my student teaching and was offered a job at a school on the west side of Chicago. The school was relatively diverse, and I was assigned a number of double-period algebra and geometry classes for students who needed more time to understand and apply basic math principles. I worked extremely hard and did my best to incorporate technology into my classes to maintain the connection to my career background. The students were generally nice, but not always engaged in learning. I also had to deal with more behavioral issues than I'd anticipated, which sometimes sidetracked the progress of my teaching. I decided to peruse the job boards and found another opportunity at the school where I'd done my student teaching the prior summer. By the following year, I was employed at a second school on the southeast side of Chicago.

This school was a better fit for me and had a more flexible schedule, allowing me to work more efficiently. But, as I experienced in the previous school, the level of engagement for some of my students continued to be a challenge. I acknowledged that mathematics did not excite others as it did for me, and I made it my mission for my students to have a better appreciation for the subject. But it was stressful to see how little some students valued education, especially given my own upbringing. In addition to their lack of engagement, many students lacked even basic mathematic skills. This was a problem, because if students could not understand the concept of adding positive and negative numbers, then teaching them algebra, geometry, or trigonometry would be even more difficult.

I spent two more years trying to find more creative ways to teach math. I played games. I found some fun computer activities that supplemented my curriculum. I brought speakers in to talk about how math is applied in the real world. I tried so many different strategies. My success was sporadic, and dealing with behavioral issues almost daily took a toll on my mental and emotional state. I had more than 150 students whose papers I graded, of which at least ten students would turn in assignments completely blank. It was heartbreaking to know that no matter how much I tried, I still had students who didn't care.

The one perk of teaching was school-free summers. I had the freedom to do whatever I wanted until school started up again and had no worries about income, since my salary was prorated over twelve months. In fact, before my second year of teaching, my husband, Tim, proposed, so I was able to spend the summers planning and executing the wedding and honeymoon. And in anticipation of having kids one day, Tim and I acquired a Pembroke Welsh Corgi puppy (that we named Oliver) when we returned from our honeymoon. It was conveniently timed to have a couple more weeks at home while Oliver transitioned to his new surroundings before I went back to work.

But I continued to struggle and felt like a failure because I couldn't inspire all of my kids. I came home increasingly sad and defeated most days, and ungraded papers always sat in my purse, which I carried with me, hoping to find some free time to grade and record them (just like how I carried my homework in high school). Some days I felt so frustrated that I let it out in the classroom. I had no desire to be around my family and friends and frequently fell asleep early on weekends due to one or two hours of sleep each night during the week. I started to wonder how I could even have a family of my own given my current mental state.

Reflecting on my career status at this point, I thought back to why I became a teacher in the first place: for a more predictable schedule. Although I had this now, I still wasn't fully satisfied. Again, I felt like I had made another bad career decision. While I didn't mind working long hours, and I was enjoying the impact I was making in some of my students' lives, the pay definitely didn't compensate for the time and emotional drain. At the end of my third year of teaching, I resigned and was left with a huge decision about what to do next.

THE MOVE TO HIGHER EDUCATION

At this point in my life, I was twenty-seven, married, and living in the city. I wanted to have my first child before I turned thirty, so it was time to reevaluate the next steps in my career. As amazed and inspired as I am by stay-at-home moms and as much as I love children, I knew that lifestyle was not in my blood, especially given the upbringing I'd had with such a heavy emphasis on career. I enjoyed interactions with others and problem solving for a common goal. I knew the next career path I pursued needed to be a job I could be passionate about. The money wasn't important anymore; I wanted a fulfilling and challenging career that highlighted my strengths because I would devote at least forty hours of my week to that job. But, I also wanted to pursue a career that allowed me to enjoy my life outside of work.

I spent that summer researching different jobs that fit my personality style. I took career tests that indicated the obvious: I'm organized, good with numbers, and like working with people. All the jobs the career assessments proposed would have required me to pursue more education, which I wasn't interested in doing. As the end of the summer approached, I was inching closer to having no paycheck, so in an act of desperation, I started applying to temp agencies.

I found out my alma mater had their own temp center, and considering my passion and commitment to the school and my experience in education, I decided to take a chance and apply there as well. Within a couple weeks, I was assigned a temp job downtown at the Northwestern law school.

This job, although temporary, was great. I worked a regular 8:30 a.m. to 5:00 p.m. schedule, went home, and didn't think about work until the next day. The work wasn't stressful, which was an unfamiliar concept for me! Since my job wasn't challenging, as an overachiever, I spent any downtime putting together more efficient processes for the department. The department was impressed with my work and wanted to hire me full time, but I ended up securing a full-time job heading a department on Northwestern's Evanston campus.

Working in this new department was probably my favorite job experience to date. The higher-education culture was definitely a slower pace than I was used to, so I was working quite efficiently. I was the "boss" of the department, and for the first time, I had the opportunity to be a real leader and decision maker. The faculty, staff, and graduate students were wonderful, and the atmosphere was extremely friendly. I was even able to bring my dog to work. My biggest accomplishment in this role was putting processes in place so the department could run more efficiently, and I started to realize my passion and talent for process improvement.

Although I loved this position, it was my first management role, and I had to learn how to transition from being an employee to being the manager. I struggled to not micromanage. As the leader, I felt I was ultimately responsible for everything, so I found myself working more hours to make sure I knew every aspect of the business in the event of a staff absence and trying to ensure the department was functioning in an optimal state and everyone was happy. I was so dedicated, I would drive into work on a Sunday before final exams if I heard the copier was jammed, which might sound crazy, but I truly cared about my department, and they reciprocated that care. I felt myself going back into my workaholic patterns from my previous jobs, but because I was appreciated for my hard work, it seemed worth it.

Two years into the role, Tim and I moved to the suburbs, and we had our first child, Justin. The department chair was completely supportive and allowed me to have a flexible schedule while transitioning back to work. However, I placed a lot of pressure upon myself and did not want to inconvenience the department, so I returned to work after five short weeks. I was definitely feeling the exhaustion of adjusting to being a new mother, while still trying to operate at the same efficiency level.

My parents cared for Justin during the day, which was wonderful because it allowed some great family bonding time between my child and his grandparents, and it was a cost savings over other childcare. But it also added an additional half hour to my commute each way. I was nursing, so my evenings were completely booked with preparing Justin for the next day. Life felt like a never-ending assembly line. To make time for all of these new tasks, my organization at home suffered. Socializing with friends suffered as well, as I was limited to chatting on the phone or seeing those who were willing to spend time with me while I was with my child.

A year later, I was ready for a new challenge and was

promoted to run a larger academic department, one that involved a larger staff, a larger research portfolio, and many more moving parts than in my previous position. This job provided me with an absolutely rich experience, and I learned department administration at an even higher level, which I enjoyed. My new department was in strong need of process efficiency, and in the two years I ran it, I was able to clear all outstanding issues and optimize the department's administrative performance. However, I was working even later hours to make sure everything was completed in a timely manner. I enjoyed the work, but my work-life balance was off.

I had transitioned my son Justin into a daycare to allow him some interaction with other children and to help lessen my commute. However, this brought the new challenge of illnesses Justin would bring home, which required me to take unexpected days off. A few months later, I became pregnant again with my second child, Ryan.

Again, I took another short maternity leave. Six weeks before giving birth, I had hired a new staff member in an essential function, and I found myself again feeling the pressure of inconveniencing the department. Even though I had a great staff to support me in my absence, I didn't want my staff to be overwhelmed. My guilt led me to choose my career over my family yet again, but I was hopeful I would bounce back quickly and balance out. We also hired a nanny to watch both boys at home and help with some of the household chores that were being neglected.

Relationships with some of the staff and faculty in my new department caused me occasional stress, and I didn't always feel appreciated. I was learning that one very important factor in my own job satisfaction was being appreciated; it was even more important than compensation. While this is not unusual—many people feel this way!—it is important to know your own job-satisfaction motivators.

After I accomplished all I felt I could in this role, I quickly started investigating my next position at the university. Being an administrator for an academic department required having the ability to wear many hats. And while I clearly enjoyed the variety, I was most interested in the financial aspects of my job. In my search, I found an opportunity to work in a financial role at Northwestern's business school under someone whose work I admired, so I took a leap into a new position.

THE JOB THAT CHANGED EVERYTHING

Now I was working in a newly created finance position that allowed me to help craft the scope of my role. I was no longer a manager; I was ready for a break from management and willing to take assignments. I could view the organization from the schools within the university level, rather than from the higher department level, which added a new layer of experience. I worked with several units in the business school I was unfamiliar with, and that gave me a clearer insight about the university. I was excited to learn more and interact with many people.

I had an amazing boss, and we worked well together. She prioritized her own work-life balance and showed me that I could actually unplug and take a vacation without feeling the pressure and guilt of work piling up in my absence. She also had a child, and it was great to have an understanding boss who was extremely supportive of my need for flexibility. I realized I had been missing out on this perk the past few years.

During this time, I was also elected as chair of the university's Staff Advisory Council, of which I had been a participating member and secretary the past few years. This was where I practiced my leadership skills, working with senior leaders at Northwestern, and my work was respected. My confidence was at an all-time high, and I figured that after three years in my finance role, I would be ready for bigger and better things; however, I wasn't sure what I wanted to pursue next. Upper-level positions became harder to find as I continued to progress in my career and usually were not available unless someone retired or left the university.

I had unofficially taken on a mentor who worked in a leadership development role at Northwestern outside my department, and he helped me navigate my thoughts on my career. I was so passionate about working at my alma mater that I wasn't interested in looking elsewhere. But I wanted a higher-level role that allowed me to influence decisions and make a greater impact on the university's mission, and those jobs were harder to find. My mentor challenged me with the question, "What if Northwestern isn't the place you're ultimately meant to be?" Little did I know that he was "coaching" me, and I didn't want to acknowledge that leaving the university was a possibility. However, I held the question in the back of my mind to possibly revisit later, and continued to search for positions there that interested me.

After two years, an opportunity on my team arose that was an increase in scope, and my desire to learn more and progress in my career inspired me to apply for the job. I would have the same manager and title, but increased responsibility. I was up for the challenge and was offered the Assistant Director of Financial Planning and Analysis position.

I was now taking on job functions that were previously done by my manager. She gave me the flexibility to learn the job in my own way, which was initially great. I asked questions and executed my tasks within my preferred working style, which is looking first from a granular perspective in order to produce a better overall understanding of the bigger picture. However, when it came time to present my work, she was really tough on me. I brushed it off, acknowledged the new things I learned, and refined my work for the following month. The next month was more of the same.

After several months of this, I slowly started to lose my confidence in the career I had built over the last seven years. Something felt terribly wrong, and I couldn't pinpoint the issue. Plus I was frustrated since I knew my boss had done this work successfully. When I asked her for more guidance, I sensed she was dissatisfied with my work. It seemed there was a large communication gap that was continuing to grow. Looking back on it now, my lack of satisfaction was due to being undervalued and unappreciated.

In short order, I felt my boss was actually trying to push me out of my role, and I was dumbfounded at the swift change in our relationship. When I talked to my friends about my situation, they suggested my boss was threatened by me, but I didn't want to believe it. I frequently found myself crying at my desk and went home mentally and emotionally exhausted, which was surely affecting my relationships with my husband and kids.

After ten months in that role, I fell apart. I wasn't functioning anymore, and my work also suffered. I couldn't sleep and just went through the motions at home with my children. My health was failing, and I felt like a zombie. I hit rock bottom. Even as I write this, I can't help but get emotional. This is an extremely painful time to relive.

One day, I did something completely out of character: I called in sick on a day I had a scheduled presentation. I went to the doctor, and she recommended a medical leave. I hesitated because I felt this step was destined to ruin my career, but I had to attend to my health, so I filed for a leave.

I spent the next few months in therapy and trying to rest. I was in a lot of emotional pain; some days I was sad, some days I was angry. I felt worthless, like a failure. But it was in those talks with the therapist that I learned I wasn't a failure, I was just meant to do other great things. I had simply been given the opportunity to rest for the first time in my life and figure out how to create a fulfilling career that was right for *me*. I began to realize I had absolutely no desire to return to my position or the university. After a six–week leave, I resigned and felt the weight of a ton of bricks lifting off my shoulders.

STARTING ANEW

When you hit rock bottom, there's comfort in knowing that things can't get worse. I strived to accept the fact that I let go of steady income and a progressing career path. But because my husband and I were smart with our finances, we were able to sacrifice my income in an effort to focus on our happiness as a family. Tim was extremely supportive of me during this time and never pressured me to return to work, even as I struggled with the desire to contribute to the household financially because I felt it had direct correlation to my worth, even though a part of me knew that wasn't true. For the first time, I was allowed to identify what I truly wanted from my life—not what anyone else told me to want. And that opportunity was very empowering, but scary.

In the year before I left higher education, I took an assessment called CareerDrivers® and learned that "Life-Work Balance" was of utmost importance to me. The following is taken from my particular CareerDrivers® assessment:

> "...People with Life-Work Balance as a Career Driver value that balance above all other motivational factors... Life-Work Balance driven people almost always have a multiplicity of interests, all of which demand attention... If this is their Primary Career Driver, people will be invested in ensuring that sufficient time is spent among various interests such as work and related interests, family, friends, hobbies, recreational and leisure activities, as well as study and learning. It is of overarching importance to them that no single area of life overwhelms the others. They are concerned with their total lifestyles; and how they define their lifestyle is the major guide to, and constraint on, their careers. This group gravitates towards jobs, careers and organizations that allow them the most flexibility possible to make all the areas of their lives work together in a balanced whole."

I continued to take assessments as part of my career development: Myers-Briggs, DiSC, and StrengthsFinder, to name a few. The key benefit assessments provide is additional perspective. While career and personality assessments don't define you, they can provide important insights about how to more effectively utilize your innate skills, strengths, and motivators. Through these assessments, I gained awareness about my personality and attitudes about life, which allowed me to make better decisions on how I interact with myself and others. The CareerDrivers® assessment, in particular, reiterated my need for a balanced life—one that was fulfilling not only at work, but outside of work as well.

As I started to deeply reflect, I realized that I had allowed my career to dominate my life, and that did not make me happy. While I had a loving family, I was always so exhausted that I rarely appreciated my time with them. I recall my kids poking at me, trying to get my attention while my brain was still in work mode, and I would divert them to the television because I had no energy. Then I recalled my youth, and how I wished my parents were more available, and I realized that I was depriving my children of that deep connection I'd wanted with my own parents. I was not willing to continue giving priority to my work over my family, so I knew my next steps in life would need to address that.

As for my other priorities, I realized all the different career paths I'd taken over the past decade had actually helped me identify what was truly important: I wanted to be of service to others and be appreciated for my gifts. I wanted to be intellectually challenged, thinking at a strategic level and determining efficient action plans toward great accomplishments. I wanted to work with people, and I needed flexibility and control of my schedule. Each of my previous jobs had been missing one or more of these important things, and ignoring my priorities had led me to feel unfulfilled.

When I thought about possible careers to align with these priorities, one word came up that was scary for me: Entrepreneur. *What product or service I could provide? And I've never done anything like this before.* I also knew that starting my own business would mean a lot of work and potential lack of income for a while. For thirteen years, I'd taken the safer route of picking jobs I was good at. And while that was fine at the time, I learned that while I felt "safe," I wasn't truly happy.

While trying to figure out the next steps in my life, I finally had time to address things I had been neglecting. I reorganized my house and got rid of clutter that was building since I'd had my children. I planned vacations. I took the kids to activities and spent much more quality time with them. I cooked meals, and we had dinners as a family. I exercised regularly and socialized frequently. I even took some time to relax and binge watch television shows, something I hadn't done in years.

WHY LIFE COACHING?

After a few months of what I called "bumming around," I finally decided to look into the profession I felt would be my dream job: life coaching. I initially resisted this option because it wasn't engineering, law, or medicine. I also had little exposure to personal development; I had no idea who people like Tony Robbins or Wayne Dyer were. I feared it might be too "woo-woo" for me, as I was a logical thinker. However, when I finally researched coaching certification programs, I realized that helping people streamline their lives to achieve balance and happiness was a form of coaching. Plus, I was already an efficiency expert in my previous career, so I signed up for a program within weeks.

In the following nine months, I experienced an unbelievable personal transformation. I allowed myself to be completely vulnerable and explored everything that had held me back for years. I always knew I was efficient, but, suddenly, my productivity was shooting through the roof. My confidence bounced back to an all-time high. I learned to truly love myself and stand up for what I wanted and needed in life. It was an emotional roller coaster, but absolutely worth it. Everything I thought was impossible before was now within my reach. I gave positive energy to the world and I attracted it, as well. I embraced my authentic self, and those who knew me watched my mindset completely shift. As I finished my coaching program, I hired my own business coach to support me in my entrepreneurial efforts. I started attracting clients immediately; my business took off, and I was officially an entrepreneur.

It is amazing to have a career that is challenging, one that I am truly passionate about. I am fulfilling my desire to help others and being appreciated for my gifts. And most importantly, I have can set my own rules and hours, and redefine success on my own terms.

My mentor had been right: ultimately, Northwestern wasn't the best place for me. I didn't want to admit it at the time, but it makes perfect sense now. And although I had to endure a wide variety of experiences and emotions in order to get to where I am now, I don't think I would have been able to truly understand the pains of an unbalanced life, nor would I be able to help others navigate toward having their own balance.

And this is when the fun really starts...

three

FUN AS A VALUE

The first time I did a webinar for my business, I was fearful about whether my content was good enough and that the attendees would feel it was worth an hour of their busy lives. It had been nine years since I presented in a teaching capacity, and while I'd done a handful of presentations over the years, this was a new and unique experience. I would be teaching content virtually and couldn't gauge the recipients' reactions in real time. All I could share with my audience was a PowerPoint presentation, my voice, and my energy.

In that first webinar, I addressed how people could make more time to do the things they love without sacrificing their career success—in other words, how to have more fun. Putting together the presentation slides initially seemed like a teeth-pulling activity. I found myself bored with my content. My anxiety about whether or not I could execute this successfully started to rise. I almost wanted to give up and quit. Then, I asked *myself* what I loved to do and how I could do more of it. I reminded myself that having fun was the driver for how I live my own life, and I realized in that moment that I wasn't walking the talk. I quickly shifted my thinking and got back to work.

I looked at my boring slides again. Since I enjoy comic relief, I thought of an app that created funny images of an avatar designed to look like me and started embedding them into my slides. I laughed hysterically while sitting at my computer. I thought about how the webinar platform I was using had boring elevator-style music while waiting for the webinar to begin, so I found different music that was happier, upbeat, energetic, and modern, and used those songs instead.

Leading up to the webinar, instead of trying to keep calm and watch the clock count down, I blasted some music I loved and danced and sang loudly instead of worrying. I was having so much fun. And once the webinar began, I was in my element. The time breezed by and when it was over, I felt amazingly content and confident I could do it again. I received feedback that my information was refreshing, inspiring, and easy to digest. Perfect!

I'm sharing this story to show the importance of being aware of your values and the impact they make on fulfillment and happiness. Fun is something I now strive to integrate into every aspect of life: my family, career, relationships, and health and well-being. Not only do I want it for myself, but for everyone else, too; I truly am most inspired when I see others having fun. The energy that having fun brings is infectious, and how amazing would the world be if more fun existed? The minor adjustment I made in creating that webinar—aligning the task with my value of fun—was a game changer. I was able to make this task on my to-do list more of an occasion than an obligation. I pushed past my fears and took corrective action. This chapter dives into how I leverage the value of fun and infuse it into my life and work to create more balance.

WHAT IS FUN?

The dictionary defines fun as "something that provides mirth or amusement." While that is true, I wasn't inspired by that definition. So I solicited help from my friends to help add some flavor to its meaning:

> "A state of bliss in which you are completely unaware until later…when your jaw hurts because you were smiling for so long. ALWAYS follow your bliss!"
>
> –Dave C. and Susan L.

> "Fun is escape from my everyday world. Getting lost in another world of a book, play, or movie. It can be novelty, something I've never seen or done before, but it can also be something I've done many times."
>
> –Barbara H.

> "Hanging out with family and really great friends, having some drinks and really good conversation and good hearty laughs—the ones that really take your breath away."
>
> –Rebecca K.

"A vacation someplace warm where I am waited on: no cooking, no cleaning, no work, and no worries in the world."

–Elaine H.

"Legos, swimming pools, TV shows, and of course the iPad."

–My son Justin

My definition of fun is feeling extreme joy and passion as a result of experiencing new things, deeply connecting with those I love, and accomplishing great things for myself and the world.

It's important to acknowledge that similar to the term "work-life balance," the word "fun" is another subjective term that means different things to different people. While I enjoy thrill-seeking activities, such as flying trapeze and circus arts, another person may prefer gardening. While I have so much fun attending stand-up comedy shows, others may be passionate for the opera.

It's also important to know that as you grow and evolve, your definition of fun changes. As a child, my definition of fun was playing with toys and reading books. As a teenager, fun was going to the mall and talking on the telephone with friends. As a young adult, it was navigating the "real world" on my own, earning my own money, and starting my own family. At present, I'm constantly thinking about how I can take fun to the next level.

HOW TO INFUSE MORE FUN INTO YOUR LIFE

Sometimes it's easy to get lost in the motions of life and your to-do list. And while some of the things we have to do in life are not always fun, we have to work at ensuring that we balance those things by doing things that *are* fun. Here's a simple three-step process toward infusing more fun into your life *right now!*

STEP 1:

Create a list of the activities you consider fun and why.

As I mentioned earlier, fun is defined by you and only you. Become aware of the things/activities you consider fun, and then ask yourself *why* they are fun. As an example, take a look at some of the activities on my list:

a) **Travel**: When I think of travel, I think of vacation. Who doesn't love a vacation? Because I am so deeply rooted in Chicago, traveling allows me the opportunity to temporarily live in a different culture with new scenery; it gives me the occasional break I need from my comfortable home base. I can take advantage of things that I would not otherwise be able to experience. I love that travel allows me to connect with the family and friends I don't get to see every day because they live elsewhere. And when I return, I am able to appreciate my home even more.

b) **Thrill-seeking activities**: There's something about doing things others may consider crazy and not normal that lights me up. For example, I love theme parks and roller coasters. I love healthy competition.

I have been skydiving. I enjoy doing things that people assume I can't do. It's almost like my badge of bravery. The fear creates adrenaline, and after I complete the activity, I somehow feel at peace. It's almost giving me permission to feel the wide range of emotions that somehow keeps me grounded.

c) **Fantasy football**: This is something I've been doing for many years; it allows me to channel my inner tomboy. Not only that, the community and connection it gives me to those in my league is a great feeling. My brother also loves this activity, and the team we share has been a great bonding tool for us. We strategize which lineups would maximize our opportunity to win in any given week, and we agonize together when our players are injured, despite the very different and busy lives we lead. While I've never been able to secure a championship, this is a seasonal and repetitive activity that gives a refreshing feeling of hope each September.

d) **Music, theater, and movement**: These activities tap into my creative side. I enjoy singing, dancing, acting, and circus arts, as well as watching others perform. There is something wonderful about being able to express yourself in a different way that shows another dimension of you. One of my favorite activities, watching stand-up or improv comedy, also falls into this category. I believe that laughter is the greatest natural medicine, and I love the way my facial muscles hurt after an hour of comic relief.

These activities are also the ones I am not afraid to engage in alone. If need be, I am happy to attend a concert or comedy show by myself.

e) **Cheerleading**: Cheering has grown with me throughout my life, from when I was a young girl in elementary school, to being on television as a college cheerleader, to then coaching my own team. The visual nature of this athletic activity, similar to that of circus arts and flying trapeze, makes a workout look cool. In addition, there's the concept of cheering someone on—encouraging people to give their all to a task, while also being the support rock when things aren't going quite the way they envisioned—that completely resonates with me and my values. When I graduated from college and cheerleading ended, I felt like a big piece of my identity had faded. I didn't know how to replace it because I did not aspire to be a professional cheerleader. However, I've realized that after years of trying several different career paths, a life coaching career was *exactly* the way to revive this cheerful spirit within me. It's absolutely fulfilling and fun to help my clients achieve what they truly want in life, while being their cheerleader along the way.

f) **Science, technology, and mathematics**: As a former engineer, I geek out on all things tech. I once aspired to be a master of the digital technology age. The nature of logic fascinates me and requires precision; both are passions of mine. One of my fondest college memories was spending an entire weekend soldering together a digital circuit replica of an alarm system. In my first build, I made a mistake, and decided to tear it completely apart and start over. While I was mad about the wasted time, I was super excited to play some more.

STEP 2:

Think about how to insert fun into all aspects of your life.
After creating your list, start brainstorming about how to weave those fun activities into more than one aspect of your life to achieve your ideal balance. For example, when I think of travel, I know that I enjoyed traveling for work when I was a consultant, but too much travel was stressful and overwhelming. I also enjoyed traveling for vacation—not only with my family, but by myself or with friends. How did I find my ideal balance of travel? By setting the intention of traveling somewhere at least once every two months. Each trip has a different purpose that fulfills the different connections I want with my work, family, friends, and myself.

In addition, think about the common themes of what makes your activities fun for *you*. It may help to find other new and fun things you might want to try. In reviewing my list, I noticed the themes of connection, doing things that are out of the ordinary, and the general feeling of happiness and peace. If there is an opportunity to try something new that aligns with any of these things, I feel encouraged to say *yes!*

STEP 3:

Execute and observe.

Fun won't happen without the execution phase. In other words, just thinking about bungee jumping isn't the fun part; you actually have to do it, and that may take some planning on your part. In order to master a balance of fun, you need to be extremely aware of what works and what doesn't work as you execute your plans. Once you bring awareness to those observations, you can make adjustments as needed. Make sure you're not placing judgment on the things that don't work because these are the things that will give you the opportunity for more fun down the road.

Going back to the travel example, I usually plan my travel calendar well ahead of time, based on the pockets of opportunity when travel can most easily occur for me and/or my family, and I commit to those dates. Most of the destinations are based on where our friends and family live, but others are driven by a specific activity or a significant event. Usually, other opportunities for travel arise, and I try to keep enough flexibility in the calendar for that reason. However, this occasionally causes some months where I may be traveling too much, at which point I consciously have to balance that with a period of no travel. And in order to avoid that overwhelming feeling of getting back into the swing of regular life after a nice getaway, I make sure to keep my schedule light whenever I return from a trip to catch up on whatever has piled up while I was out having fun.

UP-LEVELING THE MEANING OF FUN FOR THE FUTURE

I'm not going to lie; while this chapter was the one I was *most* excited to write, I struggled to get it moving. I realized it was because, at the time, I was making yet another transition in my life—shifting my focus from the journey of becoming an amazing coach to the journey of becoming an amazing entrepreneur. While very exciting, this was the time when those two phases of my life were intersecting in a big way. I had hired a business coach two months before finishing my life-coaching program, and some of the business decisions I had previously made did not completely align with the vision my business coach had for me.

But due to my need to fulfill my commitments, I decided to figure out how to manage it all, while trying to remain centered and balanced. I was mindful of practicing what I preached. I monitored my tendency toward overcommitment by allowing myself flexibility with some of my plans and delaying and/or canceling some of my self-imposed deadlines. It was helpful, but I still sensed a tension that I couldn't quite shake. I found myself procrastinating my writing because I felt like I wasn't in the right headspace. How could I write about fun when I wasn't really having fun at the time?

Days after receiving my coaching certification, I attended my first business retreat. I was excited but scared, as I was about to learn a complex new business strategy and knew that would take a lot of effort. I was ready to dive in, but I put up some resistance because I had become protective of my time. During the retreat, I had a significant emotional meltdown when I hit my point of information overload.

I soon realized that this was a recurring pattern in my journey—hitting a low before hitting the high, much like when I created my first webinar—but I didn't like that about myself. I knew this process was the conduit for my major breakthroughs and growth, but I couldn't stand feeling inefficient when my emotions took a downswing. In those moments, I experienced a loss of control and wasn't able to immediately calm myself. Intellectually, I knew what needed to be done, but I couldn't execute.

This specific "meltdown" was actually a breakthrough moment for me because it forced me to completely accept and embrace this uncomfortable aspect of myself, and a sort of creative genius kicked in. I started to remember all the things I'd told myself on my coaching journey: life is too short; there's no more time to play small; it is my time to go big or go home. And, miraculously, everything started to shift.

I visualized the path I was working toward, one I could never see before. And even though part of that path was blurry, I was suddenly confident that I was actually *creating* my destiny. What I wanted was within my reach, and my mindset shifted into believing that I was going to make it happen. The journey invigorated me rather than triggering buried fears, and all I saw ahead of me was fun. Simply allowing myself to embrace the fear, tears, and shame—and letting it all go—was my catalyst to greatness. It was such an empowering feeling.

I realized that this phase of my life, combined with every other phase of my life, was like riding an exciting roller coaster, my never-ending thrill-seeking activity. And if I let myself scream, laugh, and be afraid while I experienced it, rather than resist it, I would achieve the level of effortless success I desired and *be* that representation of what is possible. I recalled becoming a mother and fearing my individuality was destined to be lost, but I made it a priority to defy those odds. I recalled quitting my job and letting go of financial security, and the result was creating a business I truly loved.

I decided that from that point on my definition of fun was going to be more than just a feeling. Fun was something I could and would actively create. I was going to act in unending determination, be relentless, and fight for what I wanted and knew I deserved. I now embrace the ups and downs of the ride as I steadily inch toward my goals and acknowledge it is all a part of the process. I need to experience the lower points of life in order to balance my high points in life, and only good things come from allowing myself to swing the pendulum. *This* is fun 2.0, The Cheerful Mind style. And it's going to be amazingly awesome—for all of us.

four

HEALTH AND WELLNESS

Busy people often neglect their health, which is vital to their well-being and success in life. Why? One reason is that it takes a certain amount of work and dedication to maintain a healthy lifestyle. Let's face it, we can't eat chocolate and drink beer all the time and expect to have rockin' bodies, right? We have to be mindful of how we fuel ourselves on a daily basis. And sometimes eating healthy doesn't always taste amazing, or the prep time for making healthy meals is more than the time we have available.

What about sleep? When you have so much stuff to do, how easy is it to get a good night of rest? I'm definitely guilty of the occasional two- or three-hour night of sleep, and on those days when I forced myself to go to sleep early, my mind would spin about the work I could otherwise stay up and complete.

Oh, and exercising—if there were only more time in the day to squeeze in that important function. The other half of the battle is talking yourself out of procrastination mode and committing to it. And then, working out once or twice doesn't cut it; you have to exercise regularly to reach and maintain your desired fitness level.

Another reason is that sometimes working your butt off to be super healthy only goes so far. Everyone is different, and there's no one-size-fits-all model to looking and feeling fit. While there are existing diets and fitness plans that are proven effective, it usually takes a certain amount of trial and error to figure out which one works best for *you*, depending on your lifestyle and the genes you've inherited. Even then, that might not be a permanent solution. Also, some illnesses and unfortunate events, which are completely unrelated to how we care for ourselves, can still occur. Sadly, I've lost friends who were extremely fit far too soon to things like cancer, heart attacks, or freak accidents. Making the commitment to be healthy doesn't come with a 100 percent guarantee.

So why even try? Ultimately, taking care of yourself happens to be an essential key to stress management. Stress prevents you from having fun, and it diverts your energy away from the things you really want to accomplish. Stress has also been linked to a number of diseases, many of which could be prevented by effective stress management. Therefore, optimizing your health and well-being, primarily through fitness and nutrition, will result in less stress and increased productivity. In this chapter, I share my struggles, triumphs, and how I found my place of peace and fun with fitness, nutrition, and stress management.

WHY STRESS MANAGEMENT IS SO IMPORTANT

Stress management is such a huge part of health and wellness that it is of utmost importance to both me and my clients. Due to my own experiences with stress-related issues, I have spent a good deal of time learning about and practicing effective ways to manage stress and become healthier in the process. I spent many years ignoring my stress—thinking I was invincible—until I received a clear message from my body that, in fact, I'm not invincible, and I needed to turn things around. I encourage you to keep this story in mind so it might prevent you from making the same mistakes I did.

In my last job, as communication was breaking down with my boss, I decided to apply for another position at the university to resolve my stressful situation. I was granted an interview that happened to be the same morning as a dermatologist appointment I had scheduled six months earlier. Luckily, I am good at time management, so I was able to attend this annual check-up and still arrive at my interview on time.

During that appointment, I excitedly told my doctor about the new job opportunity while she checked my scalp. It seemed odd that she was even checking it because she had never done so in the ten years I had been seeing her, but I just let it go. I continued to share other updates on how things were going in life, and when she finished, she said, "So! Tell me what's going on back here," while tapping the back of my head.

I looked at her in confusion. "What do you mean?" I had no idea what she was talking about.

She replied, "Okay, don't freak out," as I sat, trying to calm the screaming in my mind. "It appears you have a pretty significant bald patch on the back of your head. Have you been stressed?"

In that instant, a visceral shock wave went through my system. *Holy cow, was I that stressed*? I had just had my hair colored a couple weeks before, and my colorist didn't mention it. I knew I had been losing a lot of hair in the shower, but it didn't appear to be coming out in big chunks. I was crying almost every day at work and feeling super exhausted when I got home, but somehow I'd ignored it. I replied with "I guess so," then asked her how big it was. She measured it at 2.2 inches in diameter and snapped a picture for me.

She told me the bald patch was the result of a genetic autoimmune disease called alopecia areata, which was enhanced by stress. I remember my father having occurrences of alopecia areata a few years earlier, so that seemed to make sense. She also told me that there was no cure, but ongoing stress would worsen it, so I needed to start minimizing my stress. Knowing that I had to run to my interview, I scheduled a follow-up appointment and moved on with my day. I kept focused and had a great interview, but the harsh reality that stress was *literally* making me lose my hair hit me hard. I knew I needed to make some changes.

Over the next month, the bald patch grew bigger to 2.6 inches in diameter. Luckily I had long hair, so I could cover it up, but I remember my husband pointing out to me on our

New Year's vacation in California that he could see it while walking behind me. That was devastating. Several weeks later, I finally threw my arms up, went on medical leave, and eventually quit that stressful job. And magically, shortly after my last day at work, my hair started growing back.

The next few years included spending significant amounts of money and time trying to regrow my hair and manage my stress. The initial large patch completely grew back, but smaller bald patches followed. These additional patches were, luckily, never as large as the first, but I had to take daily supplements and medications and visit the dermatologist every six to eight weeks for scalp injections. To this day, some still continue to show up from time to time, even though I have successfully decreased my overall level of stress. Alopecia areata may be something I have to live with the rest of my life, but it taught me that most situations are not worth stressing over. And I'm constantly grateful that this was the scenario I was given to learn this lesson, rather than another more serious health issue. Due to this experience, I place a high priority on my health and encourage you to make sure it's part of your work-life balance.

FINDING YOUR FITNESS SWEET SPOT

When I was young, I was a wimp. I have vivid memories of playing dodgeball in elementary school and being the last girl standing on my team because I was quick on my feet and had pretty good reaction time. But then one of the guys with the strongest arms in our grade would usually be on the opposing team and chuck the ball *so hard* at me that I cried in pain. In basketball, I was the short point guard who had the worst aim and was voted most likely to miss a basket, having only scored a whopping two points in two seasons. I also took ice skating lessons and was on the cheerleading team, but I hated falling on the ice. I stayed away from any tumbling or gymnastics. The only things I was remotely proud of back then were running sprints and setting the class record for the number of sit-ups done in a minute. Otherwise, I was pretty weak.

At fourteen, I decided to continue with cheerleading at my high school, which was a rigorous program, but I also began Tae Kwon Do. My brother (who was nine at the time) had signed up, and it was so much fun watching him that I had to try it myself. There was something empowering about being able to punch and kick, defying the previous wimpy version of myself by proving I could break boards, spar against someone twice my weight, and be unbothered by a swift kick in the face. I worked my way up to a black belt after two years, and it was the first time I truly felt "athletic." I was actually asked to continue Tae Kwon Do at a competitive level, doing forms, because I had exceptional technique, but I decided to prioritize my social life and continued with cheerleading instead.

Cheerleading in college was a lot of work, but extremely rewarding; it required about twenty hours of exercise per week of weight lifting, cardio, practices, and games. I was in pretty darn good shape, but when college ended, a big part of my fitness regimen died. I struggled to find an equivalent program that kept me excited. I worked out at a gym for a couple years, but was bored and unmotivated. I started taking different classes and eventually fell in love with Pilates due to the focus on core strength, but my consultant lifestyle prevented me from being able to attend consistently. I skied a couple times and, while I loved it, it was an expensive workout. I tried golf, and although fun, I was impatient with my slow progress and lack of power and aim.

While I was a teacher, I stopped working out. I had no desire to be active because work completely consumed my life, and I was exhausted. This continued for another *six* years throughout my pregnancies and early mom years. I neglected myself terribly. For two years I talked about how much I needed to work out, but couldn't motivate myself to do a darn thing because I had no energy.

When Tim and I decided we were done having children, I finally had a reason to get back on the bandwagon. Being sedentary for so long meant I had to work hard to get back into decent shape. And not only did I get back into decent shape, but the *best shape of my life.* How did I do it?

I started by signing up for some small-group and private Pilates sessions, in lieu of a personal trainer or a scheduled group class, because I knew I didn't love exercising at the gym and group classes rarely aligned with my schedule. It was great having more focused attention on the areas I wanted to improve, and I also liked having someone to hold me accountable for my progress. Then, I added a number of different thirty-day fitness challenges that were no cost, less time-consuming, consistent, and gave me specific goals to meet. I added running and ran my first ever races, starting with 5Ks and working my way up to half marathons. I enjoyed being able to throw on some music and let my mind relax while getting a good workout, and it was gratifying to push myself to run 13.1 miles, something I never thought possible.

Next I found circus arts, namely flying trapeze. *This* was the thing that reconnected me to my cheerleading roots, the opportunity to perform, interact with others, and have fun while getting a good workout. I had to play around with the combination of all of these fitness activities to find the right balance for me. I definitely burned myself out on occasion. However, it was necessary to experience those wide swings in order to find the most effective exercise program for me.

The other thing I realized is that my exercise program can't be monotonous; I get bored easily. Many people feel this way. I usually reevaluate my workout plan every two to three months and decide what still works for me at that time. Sometimes I work out three or four times a week, but other times I take a break and only work out once a week. I pay attention to what my body tells me and do what feels right without feeling guilty.

I have met so many prospective clients who struggle to find their motivation to initiate a consistent workout routine that provides the results they seek. So let me share a few tips on how to create an exercise program that you can absolutely love and stick with:

- **Identify the areas of your body you want to improve.** Which areas do you want to focus on improving? Are you looking to increase muscle mass? Trying to get a little leaner? Want more flexibility? Want to focus on your midsection, legs, or arms and shoulders? Or do you just want a full-body workout? After identifying your fitness goals, you'll know which types of exercises or programs will best achieve them.

- **Identify how much exercise you can fit into your schedule that will also provide actual results.** An ideal exercise schedule is three times a week for twenty to thirty minutes. However, depending on your schedule and where you are in this fitness puzzle, you may elect to do more or less; it varies from person to person. Does your schedule allow you to do a little bit every day? Or would you prefer longer workouts with less frequency? Pick something that works for you, and COMMIT to it. Just make sure you're committing to something that will actually produce the results you want.

- **Figure out what types of exercises you most enjoy.** There are *so* many different kinds of exercises and programs to choose from. Some people like to exercise solo, while others prefer a buddy. Some need a structured class. Some people want a group format, others one-on-one instruction. Some people don't want to break too much of a sweat. Others want to feel the burn at the end of their workouts. Some people want a competitive component to their workouts. This may be a trial-and-error process, but don't be discouraged if it takes a few tries to find out what works best for you. Then go for it!

- **Don't go all out during your first week.** One mistake many people make is going crazy with a new exercise regime right at the beginning. This, in my opinion, is a GREAT way NOT to sustain the routine. When you haven't been exercising as part of your lifestyle, it is something that should be gradually built up. Start simple, and once you accomplish that initial goal comfortably, up the ante. Once you reach your desired fitness level, then you can run on maintenance mode. And, of course, any time you start to feel bored, switch it up! You don't need to have a monotonous system, and you can always return to a previous type of workout when you are ready.

- **Take occasional breaks.** Sometimes, your body simply needs to recuperate. Take a one-week break every eight weeks or so to let your body heal, as you've been pushing it hard during exercise. That may sound counterintuitive, but taking a break every so often has *definitely* been helpful for me. The biggest challenge, however, is keeping the short break from turning into a long-term vacation.

- **Hold yourself accountable.** How are you going to make sure you keep up with your exercise program once you get started? There are different options, including finding an accountability partner or hiring a coach or trainer who will make sure you stay on track. Sign up for a fitness event that you can work toward, such as a race or other competition or even a performance. Get an app on your phone (for example, I have used MapMyRun), or get something like a Fitbit to track your progress. You are more likely to keep progressing when you can track measurable results.

When it comes to fitness, remember three things:

1. Know WHY it's important for you to exercise. What does regular exercise do for you? One of my clients said he knew he should be exercising, but he wasn't particularly excited about working out. However, when he realized that he wanted to be healthy and around for his children, he was much more willing to execute.

2. Align exercising with your values. Obviously, for me, it needs to be fun, and I need to feel a sense of accomplishment when it's done. Working toward a flying trapeze show, a race, or a specific result sweetens the deal for me.

3. Think about how you might multitask exercising with other areas of your life. For instance, when I ski, I am also having fun on vacation and spending time with my family. At a trapeze class, I get to socialize with my friends there. And I even created a team for a Spartan race called "The Cheerful Mind" that incorporated my friends, business, and fitness at the same time. *This is how you get more stuff done and have more fun!*

NUTRITION AND HEALTH

For busy people, nutrition can be an area that is just as hard to tackle as fitness. Again, each person has his/her own needs and they vary by person. I have struggled with finding the time to eat well. Partly, I knew that my metabolism was high, and I could get away with eating poorly at times, but I also always considered healthy meals time-consuming or expensive ordeals. And, unfortunately, as a person who was always on the go, I rarely ate breakfast; I dined out frequently and had absolutely no desire to cook. I would feel guilty any time people asked me what I ate because I wasn't eating kale salads and quinoa every day. When I became a mother, it was more apparent that I needed to be more health conscious for the sake of my family. I felt like I was not the best role model for healthy eating, and it stressed me out. I knew something needed to change, and I had to keep some things in mind when it came to healthy eating:

- I had no desire to completely cut out *everything* that was considered "unhealthy." I do not subscribe to fad diets that limit me from eating things I think are delicious. I enjoy pizza and hamburgers and French fries, and you can bet I still eat them occasionally.

- I knew that I would still be dining out. I enjoy having food made for me on the spot and spending little time thinking about it.

- I wanted to start cooking more, but didn't want it to be time consuming and kill my productivity in other areas.

- I'm not a fan of leftovers, so I needed to learn how to cook appropriate portions.

- And finally, I was aware that feeding a family required an awareness of my husband's and kids' needs, as well my own. While I need to consume carbohydrates and protein to keep my energy levels up, my husband would benefit from eating fewer carbs, and my children were relatively picky.

What resulted was a family nutritional system that gave me a little bit of everything. I found a meal delivery service that packages and sends all the fresh ingredients and recipes for three different healthy meals (of my choice) per week for me to make. [Note: I currently subscribe to HelloFresh, but there are similar services, such as Plated and Blue Apron, out there, too.] I also purchase groceries for the house, which includes a combination of fresh foods and snacks for consumption during the week. And when we feel like eating at a restaurant, we dine out, mostly targeting healthier meals, but I'm also open to a quick fast-food meal if our schedule requires it. When shopping for groceries is too time-consuming, I take advantage of online grocery websites that deliver items to the house and maximize my efficiency.

At one point, I worked with a health coach to explore my relationship with food and gain awareness about how food consumption affects my energy and how different types of foods affect me. I was also able to identify healthier alternatives for snacking, and some other options for cooking quick and healthy meals for myself and my family. Although I didn't drastically change my eating habits as a result, I was able to address my nutritional concerns and find a plan that felt right for me.

The important takeaway here is that everyone needs to find the method that works best for their needs. Sure, I am always trying to be mindful about what I'm putting into my body, but my current system is what feels most balanced to me. Others may choose to completely stay away from fast-food places like McDonald's, and that's great! I will eat a Big Mac *on occasion*, and as long as I don't feel any guilt, that is the main issue.

OTHER STRESS MANAGEMENT STRATEGIES

Stress management can be quite challenging, but it is essential to your health and well-being. While fitness and nutrition are among the most important tools to use, there are a number of other practices and things to consider in decreasing your overall level of stress. For instance, getting enough sleep is also very important. Busy people have a tendency to run on all cylinders throughout the day, which, without adequate rest, will negatively affect us physically, mentally, and emotionally. Sleep is the time when your body gets to slow down and build up energy for the following day.

Have you ever gone to sleep really late and woken up early feeling sluggish, reaching for a cup or two of coffee just to make it through the day? As you think about work-life balance, also consider a "sleep-awake" balance. The recommended time for sleep is approximately seven to nine hours a night, depending on your age and genetics. When you don't allow yourself that time, your body will eventually force you to play "catch up" (such as sleeping for ten to twelve hours, or taking naps), or it will send you a different signal that could manifest as a more serious health issue.

I always encourage my clients to get adequate sleep, and it is helpful to be aware of how many hours you are getting per night. I use my Fitbit as a sleep tracker, and when I am cranky, I can always check my sleep logs and know why. Usually when I sleep fewer than six hours, I know I'm going to need coffee. But when I sleep seven, I can have a productive day without it. Again, everyone has different sleep needs, but you can easily tell whether or not you are getting the sleep you need.

Other techniques to manage stress that I have tried include:

- **Meditation:** This practice didn't excite me, but when I kept an open mind, the first time I tried it, I found "The Cheerful Mind." Now when I feel tense, nervous, or afraid, I take a few deep breaths and clear my mind. Sometimes I will lean on a friend to lead me through a guided meditation.

- **Yoga:** As an alternative to silent meditation, it's a form of active meditation that can one can do to multitask with a workout, which is always a plus!

- **Acupuncture:** This is a component of traditional Chinese medicine (TCM) that addresses a wide range of conditions, but can be effective for stress management as well. What I feel is great about this method as an alternative to meditation is that you are generally forced to lie still (and you definitely don't want to mess with the needles!) and you can even get a little bit of extra sleep.

- **Massage:** Stress is often felt in the muscles, especially after prolonged exercise. A massage promotes relaxation and well-being, and relieves that tension.

- **Chiropractic:** Usually people consider this form of alternative medicine primarily to address back pain, but it also is a form of stress management because if your body is misaligned, that negatively affects your mental and physical states and prevents you from being productive.

There are surely other methods of reducing stress, but again, it's important to find which method works best for you. Try a few different techniques and notice what works and what doesn't, depending on your situation. And most importantly, remember that stress can never be completely eliminated. But actively working to accommodate and adapt to it will set you up for success.

Looking back on my life, I realize that I've created a lot more stress than was necessary. I frequently set a high bar for achievement due to the pressure of needing to be successful. I wanted to control every outcome, and when I didn't get the result I wanted, I was unhappy. When I neglected my health, I lacked the necessary energy to maximize my productivity and my happiness. Even though it has required much patience and perseverance on my part, I ultimately found that all I *really* wanted was to take advantage of the life I was given and be happy and healthy for my loved ones.

Once I made the commitment to find balance in my health and well-being, I found a level of happiness and vitality I had never experienced before, and those who know me best notice the difference.

five

MONEY MANAGEMENT
STRATEGIES

In this chapter, I share my story and some tips that may help you make the most of the money you have and how your mindset can help create more wealth. As a former finance professional and math teacher, I'm an absolute numbers geek, which means managing my finances is something I'm naturally passionate about and is, coincidentally, an important part of the work-life balance equation. While the amount of money we have plays a role in our overall comfort in life, it's not the solution to all problems.

The saying "Money doesn't buy happiness" is true. Sure, having a good amount of money can minimize stress, but conversely an abundance of it doesn't determine your ultimate level of success or satisfaction in life. That said, it is still important to understand the value of money and how you can leverage it to maximize your happiness by achieving your goals. Before we get started, I want to remind you that I am not a financial advisor, nor am I making any specific recommendations. While I will discuss some general, well-known money management strategies, I suggest that you consult with a professional to find the strategies that will work best for your particular situation.

MY STORY

When I was growing up, money was tight. As I mentioned earlier, my parents came to the United States from the Philippines and worked their butts off to have a comfortable life. Even as a young child, I was taught the importance of utilizing money wisely. For my parents, it was important to spend only on necessities and things that were in alignment with their top values. We always shopped for bargains and never wasted food. Due to my parents' experiences and the hard work they put into earning those dollars, they encouraged me to live within my means and instilled a "saver's mentality" in me.

Because my parents placed such high value on education, they didn't allow me to work a job when school was in session. This was frustrating for me because most of my friends were working, and I wanted to make money that I could spend on things I wanted. Instead, my parents were supportive when I wanted something, and as long as I could justify the benefit for the purchase, they were willing to make an investment. To help me learn my own money management, my parents gave me a weekly allowance to cover expenses for school lunches, and any remaining cash at the end of the week could be used for whatever I wanted, which I rationed accordingly.

In addition, I was financially rewarded for my hard work when I produced good grades in school. More specifically, if I made the honor roll in an academic quarter, my parents rewarded me with $100. If I received straight A's (something I strived for but rarely accomplished), I would get $500. The interesting caveat for that money was that although I'd "earned" it throughout my elementary and high school years, I didn't have full access to it until college. The money was placed in a savings account under my name, and I periodically went to the bank with my dad to deposit any gift money and the earnings from my good grades. In those visits, he taught me how to submit deposits to the teller and how to balance a checkbook so by the time I started college, I was completely prepared to manage the account on my own.

There were definite pros and cons to this strategy. One of the benefits was it incentivized me to work extremely hard and make my education a priority. It also taught me a *huge* lesson about the importance of saving and managing money. However, a downside I realized much later in life was that I subconsciously tied my worthiness to money (i.e., A's were worth more than B's, etc.). As an adult, I felt I had to work harder in order to make more money, and if I wasn't making a salary that was high enough, I saw myself as a failure. In some ways, the strategy my parents chose worked well for me, but didn't serve me in others.

As a parent, I also have to consider how to teach my young children about money management, and still I think about these pros and cons I experienced. I started to teach my kids early about the value of money and how to spend it. One strategy we tried was rewarding our kids with one dollar each day they made overall good choices (as determined by my husband and me) and added it to a "virtual bank." Whenever we went shopping, they could use their accrued money to purchase an item *or* save up more money to purchase a higher-priced item later (delayed gratification). This system not only helped raise awareness about the cost of toys, but also helped my children prioritize what they truly wanted. I also opened bank accounts for my boys at an early age and, just as my parents did, I deposit any gift money they receive there, which they can access when they are older. However, I do want be mindful about the dangers of tying one's self-worth to money, so I might think twice before implementing a money-based behavioral rewards system as the kids get older.

I have tried many different strategies when it comes to managing my own money, and it's important to note that it is a process of both logistics and mindset. As your life situation changes, your strategies usually need to change as well. To effectively manage your money, it's important to be aware of your current situation, understand your goals, and put together an action plan. As you execute the strategies, observe the outcomes and adjust your plan as needed. What I share next are some of the things I've learned along the way that have helped me find financial success.

WISE SPENDING HABITS

Let's talk about effectively spending your hard-earned moolah! Doesn't it frequently feel like we have to work hard to earn the dollar, but when it comes to spending, it's insanely easy? And there's so much stuff out there to buy or do! Some people like to splurge on clothes or accessories, tech gadgets, educational material, personal care, fancy name brands, spa days, vacations, you name it; the list is endless. Ultimately, how you spend your money is completely up to you, *but* the following are some expert guidelines that may help you spend *wisely* and *authentically*:

- Be aware of your means: It's important to know how much money you actually have to spend. While people sometimes elect to pursue lines of credit and other loans that stretch them beyond their means, try to be mindful about how often you do this and determine the actual cost of borrowing. A loan might make sense for big-ticket item purchases like cars, education, or homes, but it's not smart to use high-interest credit cards on unnecessary things—unless you can (and do) pay off your monthly balances in full to avoid the high interest charges that also compound monthly.

- Understand needs vs. wants: A *need* is an essential item that is necessary in order to live your life, whereas a *want* is something that you would like to have but don't need. Also be aware that some items can be classified as both a need and a want: for example, food is a need, but what you specifically choose to eat is often a want. If you don't actually need something you are considering buying, then make sure it's a want you can afford and will actually use.

- Determine whether it's best to spend now or spend later: Think about the urgency of the item you are planning to purchase. Let's say you are planning to buy a new computer. Do you absolutely need it now? Or can you live with what you currently have for a little while longer? Are you willing to wait for the next model to come out? Understand the "why" behind your rationale of purchasing sooner, so that you are making the best logical decision for your purchase.

- Take your values into account: Remember what my top values are? Fun and accomplishment. If what I'm buying does not align with my values, it's probably not a good purchase. Keep the following in mind when you are considering purchases:

  o Are you the type who values connection? If so, then maybe it would be more exciting to sign up for a course with a group component than just utilizing a self-study manual.

  o Do you value flexibility? Then you might want to think twice about investing in a regimented fitness program that restricts your schedule, or locking in on a one-year commitment if you have the tendency to change your mind frequently.

  o Is clarity of communication important to you? Perhaps you'd be happier hiring a landscaper who communicates clearly and provides you with detailed invoices, instead of one who just bills you without explanation.

o   You also want to keep your values in mind when you're comparing items. For example, if comfort is more important than appearance, a woman may opt to purchase a pair of cushy dress shoes over stiletto heels.

FINANCIAL PLANNING

A clear, strategic financial plan is essential to growth and maintenance of your wealth. When planning for your financial future, it's important to consider consulting with a certified financial planner (CFP) because CFPs can help you review your current situation and make solid recommendations that align with your financial goals. It is also best to seek someone with an unbiased perspective, rather than someone who is just trying to sell their company's products. As you work with your planner, think about how to leverage your finances for both the short term and the long term.

The *short term* means effectively managing your day-to-day expenses: the daily transactions you conduct, payment of your bills, and handling your liquid cash. The accounts that typically fall into this category are your checking and savings accounts and credit cards. As the money manager for my household, here are my top tips on being efficient in the short term:

1. In an effort to save time, I do *not* recommend having multiple credit cards. More accounts take up more time and increase the potential for error in paying bills in a timely manner, thus incurring late fees and additional interest charges. Having more accounts

also increases the possibility of spending more and not living within your ability to repay the balances in full, which all financial experts recommend. Fewer credit cards can also help minimize fraud and the risk of identity theft.

2. Work with as few financial institutions as possible. The ease of having all of your accounts consolidated into a few places minimizes the time you spend transferring funds between accounts, checking balances, and paying bills.

3. Set your recurring bills on auto-pay through your checking account. Not having to worry about billing-cycle due dates minimizes stress. Then you can shift your focus to ensuring you have the adequate funds to pay those bills.

4. Pay off debt every chance you get. While it's not always easy to pay down loans, the less debt you sustain means fewer bills and more incoming cash and time for other things you want to accomplish. And since high interest rates like to magically make your money disappear faster, pay off higher-interest-rate credit card balances and loans first. If you have to run a balance on a credit card for a short period of time, use a card with a low interest rate. *Bonus tip*: If you can apply for a card that has 0 percent interest for an introductory period, take advantage of it! Just make sure you pay off the full balance when it's due or you'll get hit with some massive interest charges on top of late fees.

5. Monitor your credit score. This is important because your credit rating impacts your ability to borrow money—a higher credit score will aid in securing a better mortgage rate, lower-interest credit cards, and car loans. Lower credit scores indicate higher-risk individuals (meaning people who have a history of late or missed payments) to potential lenders, who often charge people with lower credit scores more than those less-risky individuals with higher scores— or won't lend to them at all.

    In addition, a credit report can alert you to identity theft and other types of fraud. A credit report will give you a listing of all accounts created in your name. There are many options to review your credit score that are free, or, alternatively, you can invest in a credit monitoring service. (I do 3-in-1 credit monitoring with Equifax, which allows me to access to the other two major credit bureaus as well.) Some tips to increase your score include paying credit card balances in full and on time, keeping your oldest credit account open to indicate financial stability to lenders, and minimizing the number of credit inquiries to your file by only seeking credit when you need it.

6. Regularly monitor your transactions and spending habits. For most people, this means creating a budget. While I agree that a budget is important, there are varying methods of how people can budget their money, so I want to emphasize that it's important to understand your spending habits and be aware

of which transactions are hitting your accounts and when. First, continuously verify your transactions to ensure that all of the debits to your checking accounts and credit cards are indeed yours. While technology is usually accurate, issues like fraud or human keying errors can still happen, and you can more easily resolve potential problems by regularly checking the charges to your accounts. This can be as detailed as downloading an app on your phone that allows you to review transactions (such as Prosper Daily or Mint), or simply glancing through your monthly credit card and bank statements as soon as you get them. Second, when monitoring your spending habits, it's good to be aware of your spending categories (such as food, travel, child care, etc.), *and* identify the trends on how spending may change from month to month. This is important so that you can make smarter decisions about how to manage your money at different times. For example, we've noticed that for family vacations, there are generally two big spikes in spending: once when we book the airfare and again during the actual travel month. In anticipation, we will either actively plan to decrease spending in other months or put some extra money into savings to make sure we can cover all the anticipated costs.

7. Most experts recommend having at least three to nine months of living expenses in a savings account at all times for emergency situations. For busy people who don't want to add more stress to their already crazy lives, having a savings fund that you *regularly*

contribute to is a great way to easily manage funds when unexpected events arise. The following are all examples of experiences I have successfully bounced back from with minimal stress because I placed high priority on saving for unexpected events.

Our sixty-year-old house had settled to a point where the piping to the external sewer system became blocked, and the outgoing dirty water flowed back into the house, out of the first floor toilet, and seeped through the walls into the basement. Many items of value (both financially and emotionally) were ruined.

Another time, my youngest son became sick and was hospitalized while my husband and I were attending my cousin's wedding in California, so we had to leave early and book the next flight back home. Luckily, we had some money set aside to pay for these unexpected home repairs, travel expenses, and medical bills that insurance didn't cover, which meant I didn't have to stress over paying for these necessary things that I could never plan for.

Long-term financial planning actually means *preplanning* for your family's future and your eventual retirement. Having an investment and retirement strategy, while daunting because it is hard to predict the future, is important for your financial success. This includes retirement accounts (IRAs 401(k)s, 403(b)s, etc.), and college savings funds for your children. Many CFPs specialize in helping their clients with retirement planning.

While I'm not a financial advisor, the most important piece of advice I can give, which is echoed by the experts, is to start investing in your retirement *as soon as you start working*—especially for companies that match retirement contributions; you don't want to leave money on the table. The earlier you start this practice, the better, as inflation will work in your favor over the years, and you may even have the opportunity to retire at a younger age.

In addition, you may want to think about the financial legacy you want to leave behind for those you love. Creating a will can minimize stress for those who might handle your remaining assets. Whether you have few or many assets, a will is important to avoid lengthy probate and clarify your wishes. You may also want to consider life insurance as a financial security measure for those who remain after you are gone. In making sure that you address these sometimes difficult long-range plans, you and all involved will benefit from minimized stress. Again, consult a CFP to determine the best strategies for your particular situation.

TIME VS. MONEY

One important consideration when managing your finances is remembering that your time is just as valuable as cash—and sometimes even more so. When faced with a decision on how you want to resolve any given problem, it's important to think about which is more important to you: your money or your time. At what point do you decide to financially invest in something that will give you more time to focus on other things you want to accomplish?

When I first started living on my own, I lived the DIY lifestyle for anything and everything I could possibly do myself: cleaning the house, running to the grocery store, doing laundry, home improvement projects, etc. I paid only for services that were beyond my own expertise, such as resolving a plumbing or electrical issue. As my life became more complex, I started running out of time and found myself sacrificing experiences that were important to me, such as having fun with friends and family or even being happy. At that point, I became willing to pay other people to do things I used to do simply because it gave me more precious time.

The ultimate question is how much is *your* time worth? The answer can be found by again revisiting your values. If you choose to invest the time, what might you be giving up? What might you gain? Consider the trade-offs and know that the decision is yours. Others may choose a different path, and that's completely reasonable for them.

For example, when you consider commingling your finances with someone else, it's important to understand how each person views personal financial management. For example, my husband and I have very different perspectives about money, which I find interesting because we come from similar financial situations. Early on in our relationship, I realized that I was more willing to spend my time than my money to achieve certain goals. He was the opposite, preferring to spend money rather than his time. I believe that this was helpful for both of us; he helped me relieve some stress over feeling the need to pinch pennies all the time, while I helped him gain more awareness about how he allocated his funds.

When working in a partnership, it's best to craft a joint financial management style that works for both of you based on your combined values and priorities. Some couples may completely join their accounts, while others may own joint accounts but keep separate personal discretionary funds. Some choose not to commingle accounts at all. Regardless of the strategy you choose, it will be successful as long as the lines of communication remain open and there is willingness to be flexible.

ALTERNATIVE CURRENCIES TO MONEY

When thinking about money, it's good to know that more currencies exist beyond the tangible dollar (or euro, peso, etc., depending on your location). There are other ways to acquire goods and services and/or save money on what you buy. For example, free loyalty programs at select stores can save you an extra couple dollars (and are usually more efficient than paper coupons, although those are great as well).

Rewards points are another tool to help pay for the things you want. I generally suggest using a credit card that earns rewards on your transactions. You can choose from cash back, airline miles, hotel points, or reward programs at any of your favorite stores. To avoid having to pay an annual fee, there are some no-fee rewards cards, such as the American Express Hilton Honors card, or the Discover IT card.

If you want to maximize your rewards, you can alternatively sign up for a card with an annual fee (one of my favorites is the Chase Sapphire Card). The fee is generally waived for the first year, and should you change your mind and want to avoid fees, you can usually request to downgrade the card before the year is over. The reward accrual will be slower if you downgrade, and you may lose certain perks if you choose to do this. Always read the terms of each card before you apply.

One other option is to consider bartering, also called "trading," or exchange of goods or services in lieu of cash. For example, a chef may help cater a party for his interior designer friend in exchange for some assistance with his restaurant decor. When trading goods or services, it is important to understand the value of each good or service in determining a fair exchange, but it is a great alternative for purchasing the things you need.

If there is something you want that may stretch you beyond your financial means, consider these other opportunities to accomplish the same goal. Put your brainstorming hat on, get creative, and claim what you want!

MONEY MINDSETS: ABUNDANCE VS. SCARCITY

Do you ever wonder how some people go from broke to wealthy or vice versa? Believe it or not, there's a lot more to consider beyond the logistical piece of money management. Your attitude about money also directly impacts your level of wealth. The term "money mindset" means the thoughts, beliefs, and perceptions you have about finance and wealth. To explore your money mindset, take a few minutes to answer these questions:

- What initial things come to mind when you think about money?

- How much money do you need in order to be successful?

- What are your views about how others choose to spend their money?

- Is it okay to desire a lot of money?

What types of feelings came up when you answered these questions? Were they positive? Negative? While there are many different perspectives about money, I'd like to highlight the difference between having a mindset of abundance and a mindset of scarcity, and how these mindsets can impact your ability to achieve financial freedom.

When you think about not having enough money and don't believe that you can make the money you need, that is scarcity mindset. Alternatively, when you exude a more positive attitude of opportunity *and* truly believe that you can create more wealth for yourself, you lean toward an abundance mindset. The "Law of Attraction" is a concept that states: Like energy attracts like energy. The principle is the same for your positive or negative thoughts about money. If you tend to think money is scarce and very hard to come by, it will be much more difficult to achieve the wealth you want. However, if you can shift your mindset toward abundance, you can open the doors for more wealth.

Now, here's the tricky part—how do we do this? The reason it can be difficult to shift our mindset to abundance is due to the beliefs and fears we have developed over time, and they may subconsciously be preventing us from creating the wealth we all deserve. In my case, I was afraid to quit my unsatisfactory university job because I believed we needed my salary to maintain our family's lifestyle. I had worked the usual nine-to-five (or more!) for almost fifteen years, and that's all I knew; I couldn't fathom what my life would be like without a paycheck. While I knew that my take-home earnings at the time were covering all of our child-care expenses, I was also maximizing contributions to my retirement accounts and was wary about discontinuing that retirement investment. It actually took me a few months to realize that the value of my happiness was worth more than my salary, and I finally cut the cord and jumped off the cliff of traditional employment.

The first step I took to shift my mindset was clearly identifying what I truly wanted. Ultimately, I desired more happiness and fulfillment. I wanted this because I didn't want to look back at my life knowing that I just went through the motions and didn't make the most of the time I was given. I wanted a strong connection to my family, a career I could enjoy, and the freedom to live my life my way. I clearly didn't have these things, so I knew it was time to make a change—and some of my goals related directly to money.

Once I knew what I wanted, I then challenged any thoughts I held that prevented me from *believing* that I couldn't have what I wanted. I looked to people I admired and asked myself why I didn't deserve what they had. *I did!* Then I identified areas in my life that I could adjust or remove because they were not aligned with my ultimate goals. I committed to executing a plan that would keep me on the path to getting the life I wanted.

As soon as I quit my job, I began seeking opportunities. I took a good hard look at our financial spending and, recognizing that my income was eliminated, I started cutting costs everywhere for things we didn't truly need. I looked at the ridiculous cable bill that was auto-debiting from my credit card every month and spent the time to adjust our service to what we essentially needed. Because I had been so tired, we would frequently dine out, so I strategized how to cut the amount we spent on food, which entailed cooking at home now that I had more time. Gas expenses naturally decreased as a result of eliminating my commute. And I became more mindful about my spending, but I also didn't drastically change our quality of life.

After about six months without my income, I reviewed our financial situation again and noticed that we were sustaining our account balances even without my paycheck. I realized that having the extra time to do a deeper dive of our expenses became an alternative way for me to "earn" money for the family through increased savings. Because I had been afraid to take the leap, I wasn't able to create the life I wanted. As soon as I broke through the fear and committed to the life I wanted, my mindset shifted and I adjusted accordingly.

So, if you know that your money mindset can use a little adjusting, the first step is to get super clear about what you *truly* want. Then, rid yourself of any excuses or reasons why you believe you can't have it. Finally, put a plan in place to get what you want. If you hit roadblocks, brainstorm alternative solutions and get creative. This strategy will bring you closer to the wealth you want and deserve.

COMPARISON AND SELF-WORTH

In addition to shifting toward an abundance mindset, another thing to watch is whether you play the "comparison game." It is completely understandable and natural to use comparison as a benchmark of our own progress; however, it can also cause us to lose sight about what's really important. Just because the Smith family has a summer house and we don't, it doesn't define our happiness, "wealth," or lack thereof.

Keeping our values in mind will help keep us focused on our priorities.

Your self-worth can also dictate your personal wealth. When you allow your salary to define you, you limit your wealth potential. When things started to take a downturn with my former boss, my immediate reaction was that it was my fault: I wasn't smart enough or had extended myself beyond my capabilities. I didn't feel worthy enough to advance in my career or ever lead a company—just based on that one interaction. And as a result, I prevented myself from dreaming big and accomplishing more. Where would I be now if I continued to think that way? Would I be satisfied with just settling for mediocre? Would I regret never trying to find the answer? Luckily, I pushed myself out of my comfort zone, began believing in myself, and created my own successful company. If I can do it, so can you!

If you are feeling less than worthy, spend some time writing down all the ways you provide value to anyone who interacts with you. If you run out of ideas, ask other people to tell you how they are inspired by you. Increasing your confidence in the value *you* provide can actually put more money in your pocket. You *are* enough.

In summary, there are many facets of money management, and it's not solely a numbers game. One of the most important things I have learned about the topic is that there is no one perfect way to manage money. Everyone has different situations and perspectives, and they can also vary in different cultures and generations. While there are some general guidelines to follow, it's most important to understand your own situation and pick a strategy that works best for you. Then stick to it!

Knowing what is ultimately important to you and your family will help you make better decisions about how to leverage your assets. It's important to save, but it's also important to spend—perhaps even occasionally splurge. You deserve to enjoy the fruits of your labor, and you can achieve true happiness and wealth by fostering a healthy relationship with money.

six

RELATIONSHIPS

$\mathcal{All}$ relationships are unique; the bond between any two people is completely different from any two others. As humans, we have different relationships with our family, friends, significant others, work colleagues, classmates, and even pets. The dynamic of a relationship can also change as more people are added. And there's one more relationship that we tend to forget about but is absolutely the most important, which is the *relationship with ourselves*. In this chapter, I share some experiences and lessons I learned from varying relationships in my life and how I have created a healthy balance among them all.

LESSON 1: AUTHENTICITY

Doesn't everyone love a great love story? Well, let me get a little personal and tell you about my journey to finding love. I have always been a "chronic long-term dater." For most of my life, starting as early as fifth grade (yes, I know, so early!), I was generally in some sort of relationship. Since I was a child, I wanted to find my "true love," get married, and live happily ever after, following the paths of the love stories you see in movies or on television—or even being the next Disney princess.

In sixth grade, I had my first real boyfriend, with hand holding, gifts (including a cute ID bracelet), and my very first kiss. This was a really sweet young relationship, and perhaps it was the first time I felt what I thought was "love," but after 299 days (I am so embarrassed I am sharing this, but yes! I counted the days), he told me he wanted to move on, and I was *crushed*.

Probably due to the fear of being hurt again, I didn't have another longer-term relationship until high school. During my sophomore year, I started dating a popular, three-sport athlete. I was a cheerleader, and this was an interesting relationship because he was an amazingly caring and compassionate person when we were alone, but frequently a jerk to me in public. He would ignore me during the few points in the school day when our schedules matched up. I was so torn because of the differing personalities I saw. We would constantly break up and get back together.

This continued over the course of almost four years, as I struggled to let go of the relationship I had invested so much time in, always hopeful that he would change—or maybe I could adapt. My friends and family told me to end it, but I didn't listen. Looking back, perhaps this was a result of my feeling less worthy of a healthy, satisfying relationship. However, when we attended different colleges, things changed, and I gained the confidence to know that I *was* worthy of being treated better. After a lot of pain and suffering, I found the courage to finally leave.

My next relationship was with someone at the opposite spectrum of what I had just experienced: He was an intelligent, caring, and thoughtful person. He had great family and friends, and all of my family and friends loved him, as well. I thought he could potentially be "the one." However, when I raised the topic after over a year of dating, things started to fall apart. He was a year older than me, about to graduate college, and wasn't quite ready to think about long-term commitment. I started to question what I was doing wrong. He ended up breaking things off shortly before his graduation, and I was devastated.

Enter my now husband, Tim, who had been one of my best friends through cheerleading at Northwestern. We were stunt partners for the national competition routine in our junior year and spent a ton of time together. We knew all about each other's lives and relationships, and since we were both pursuing engineering majors, we had some classes together. When my relationship ended, it was Tim who cheered me up. We hung out frequently, and he made sure I didn't sulk in my dorm room by keeping me company. A few months after that split, Tim shared something that threw me completely off guard: that he had feelings for me.

I did not know how to respond. I had never thought of

him as anything more than a friend and wasn't interested in damaging that friendship. Knowing I wasn't over my ex *and* I was going to be captain of the cheerleading squad the following year, I wasn't ready to consider a new relationship, especially with him. I honestly expressed those concerns to him over some ice cream and kindly turned him down.

In the months that followed, Tim and I naturally drifted a little. He dated others, and I ended up rekindling with my ex. However, as spring approached and I was preparing for my own college graduation, that relationship still lacked commitment and I decided to end it. During the final months of college, I took a break from relationships altogether. It was time to focus on me and I cherished the remaining moments with my cheer team and friends which, of course, included Tim.

Shortly before graduation, Tim approached me again and mentioned that he still had feelings for me. We were back to spending a lot of time together as friends and we always had so much fun together, but I still wasn't sure if I wanted to cross that line. I went back and forth, but decided to give it a try—although we kept the relationship relatively quiet at first. After graduation, we spent a month apart as he visited Europe and I went to the Philippines with my family.

When we both returned to the states, we fell into a natural, drama-free, fun, and extremely communicative relationship. We spent so much of our time together through the years as friends that there was no reason to try to impress each other or be someone we were not. Tim had mentioned during college that he wasn't the type to drag out a relationship; if by the one-year mark he didn't feel it was a fit, he would end it. And I loved his transparency and honesty. Naturally, as I was passionate about one day finding my life partner, when we hit the one-year mark, I asked him where he stood, and we did not break up.

On our three-year dating anniversary, Tim had planned some fun things for us on a trip to Los Angeles to visit some friends and family. Little did I know he had been scheming a surprise trip to Hawaii instead. The morning we were leaving, he asked me to repack my bags with more beachy clothes. We arrived in Honolulu and he pulled out all the stops: He rented a convertible and we cruised around the island, eventually settling into our beach hotel. The next morning, he took me on a boat cruise where we had the opportunity to swim with dolphins, and then we headed to a spa for a couple's massage.

Worried that he was spending too much money, I asked him to tone it down (of course, as a penny-pincher, I would say that!), and he planned an inexpensive picnic on the beach for dinner. We bought snacks from a local Walmart (that's all we could find along the drive) and secured some space on a west-facing beach of Oahu to watch the sunset. That night, he pulled a ring from his pocket and asked me to marry him.

Marrying my best friend has been a wonderful ride. Looking back at all my previous relationships and how badly I wanted to just love someone and be loved, I realized I was constantly trying to mold myself to the person I was dating, rather than just being myself, hoping he would want to spend the rest of his life with me. And none of those relationships worked out. It wasn't until I decided to be my true self that the right guy who fit that mold showed up. So to sum up the moral of this long story: I encourage you to be your true, authentic self from the start! Trying to impress by being someone you are not will cause pain and confusion down the road. It is that much harder to change once you've set a precedent that is not truly you. Set it straight from the beginning! All the other parts will fall into place.

LESSON 2: MISINTERPRETATION

Have you ever been frustrated by a total miscommunication— where you think you're heading in one direction, and someone else thinks you're going in the opposite direction? When a message you send is misinterpreted, it can be painful and potentially damaging if left unaddressed. I've seen this happen time and time again in my relationships, and it's caused quite a bit of sadness, anger, and fear in my life.

As an example, one simple misinterpretation of a situation between my immediate family and our extended family led to a huge divide, leaving us feeling like outcasts and lonely for many years. There were feelings of resentment on both sides, and the relationship had deteriorated to the point that when my father was battling cancer, barely anyone reached out to support us. When I got married, there was still so much pain that my extended family wasn't in attendance. And when an aunt passed away, we learned about it from someone outside the family. It was very sad.

While this was difficult to experience, and naturally led to blame and many "he said, she said" stories from both sides, in actuality, no one was truly at fault. It was a chain of multiple miscommunications that had spun out of control. I watched my parents in pain over issues that remained unresolved for years. And I was torn because I missed my cousins and family gatherings, but I also wanted to support my own family.

Finally, I acknowledged that life is too short, and I couldn't sit back and continue to wish things were different. I was already in my thirties, and I did not want to pass along this story to the new generation of our family. Nor was it productive to remain angry and resentful. And while I cannot control the actions of others, I knew it was worth a try to take a step toward resolution. So, because family is one of my top values, I took the step of attempting to reinstate the lines of communication. I knew that in order for it to work, both parties had to be open and willing to hear each other's side of the story in a completely safe and honest space, and they were.

The result moved our family closer to going in the same direction. While things may never be how they used to be, there is much more peace now, and everyone can make new, better-informed choices about how to move forward, which is much better than no progress at all.

Whenever painful divides like this happen in a relationship, rather than stewing in victim energy or blaming each other, it's really important to ask yourself what you truly want to see as the outcome. Do you want to be reunited, or is it better to go your separate ways? Or do you just want peace? And how much—on a scale of one to ten—are you willing to take action to achieve that outcome? When you become clear on the answers to those questions, the next thing to ask yourself is what step(s) you could take to achieve that goal. If you take no action, nothing will change.

It's also a good idea to think objectively about the situation, as heated emotions can lead to inaccurate assumptions and further communication breakdown. Allow yourself to remember that sometimes a message isn't always perceived in the manner it was intended; put yourself in the other people's shoes and ask what *they* might be thinking. Is it rational? Is it reasonable? When you approach a misinterpretation from a place of love and compassion and understanding, there is more opportunity to grow toward that place of peace you seek.

LESSON 3: ACCEPTING GROWTH AND CHANGE

As I've grown older, I've experienced many changes in my friendships. In my teenage days, I had many different friends in multiple social circles: the athletes, my classmates, my theater and music friends, and my special group of girlfriends; I was friends with everyone. As my social circles grew and my schedule became more demanding, I had to be a little more deliberate about who I spent time with. I chose a subset of my high school friends to remain in contact with, while others slowly dropped off. In adulthood, some friendships were rekindled, while others drifted, and I had to reassess which relationships to invest my time in and when. This is a completely natural process, but how can it be done in a way that fosters loving relationships and connections without any resentment as people drift in and out of our lives?

I used to struggle with the "growing apart" aspect of my friendships, sometimes feeling abandoned or that perhaps one of us did something to cause the relationship to drift; I felt the need to "blame" something or someone. But the truth is, people and circumstances change and evolve, and it's completely okay and natural to grow apart. You don't need to cut each other out your lives and damage the relationship for the long term. And this doesn't mean either person is "bad" or "wrong."

To look at it from a different angle, here are a few of Apryl's Tips for working through friendship issues:

- Instead of getting angry or frustrated with a friend, assess and embrace the current situation. Ask yourself: What were the values that drew the friendship close in the first place? Have those values shifted? Once you know the answer, is it something worth making an extra effort to keep it strong? For example, for two single women who are friends, how does their relationship change when one marries, and how might the values in this friendship change in this new life phase? They can choose to make a stronger effort to maintain their previous connection, or they can choose to acknowledge and respect each other's shift in priorities.

- When you feel challenges or vulnerabilities with friends, accept the differences as an opportunity for personal growth. Of course, no two people are the same, so think about the others' experiences and how they look at life and make decisions. How does that relate to your experiences? And understanding that you can't experience everything, how might you utilize this new information? You could choose to accept them, be more understanding, and acknowledge that they are making the best decisions under their circumstances. Or perhaps realize that their values do not align with yours and respectfully walk away.

- Know that different friends serve different purposes. It's a tall order to be the be-all, end-all friend, especially when you have passions in different areas. Your closest friends will likely not have all of the same interests as you, and this is okay; in fact, it's healthy! If you're a multi-passionate person like me, you probably have different circles of friends you can discuss your interests with, such as career, sports, parenting, and fine arts.

If you are questioning whether a relationship serves you, weigh the advantages and disadvantages. It's completely natural for relationships to change and evolve throughout life. Have a conversation with your friend when it looks like it's time for the relationship to change. It doesn't always have to be negative—change is often positive as well. Both people have to feel like they are getting something from a relationship; if that can't be resolved, then it's better for everyone to be on the same page about it.

LESSON 4: TRANSPARENCY

One thing I've noticed can damage relationships, particularly in the workplace, is the impact of transparency in communication. Transparency can help build relationships and trust at every level. There's something about collaboration and transparency that can lead to some very powerful things.

On the other hand, the absence of transparency can cause many people to feel lost, unclear why they are executing certain tasks, or unable to make fully educated decisions. Employees can feel undervalued and, therefore, unmotivated. It can result in conflict when teams are not on the same page, as well.

As a leader, it is important to know that the people you represent are being heard. When I chaired the Staff Advisory Council in my last organization, I chose to share all of the decisions I made as a leader, so my team could understand the rationale behind them. They were able to trust my judgment more and to share their opinions, if they wanted. They felt more inspired to work, and we accomplished so much more because everyone was included in the process.

That said, there is that fine line which, when crossed, can lead to "too many cooks in the kitchen." Paralysis can occur if there are *too* many differences in opinion; it is the leaders who are meant to make the final decisions, after all. How do you decide when to lead on your own vs. lead as a group? In those times when there may be conflict, or you have to deal with difficult people, or make difficult decisions, here are a few things to consider for getting back to an actionable place:

1. Understand the full situation clearly, not just from your side, but from the other side as well. Take the time to reflect on the nature of the relationship between you and the person with whom you are experiencing conflict. Are you peers? Is it a manager/ employee relationship? Who is ultimately responsible for making the decision?

2. Assess all the possible outcomes and evaluate the pros and cons of each one. What is the best solution for all parties involved? Is the best solution for you aligned with the best solution for others? Which solution is ultimately the most important?

3. Be willing and open to debating the situation with them; stand your ground on the things you believe in. Find the happy mediums. If the result doesn't go in your favor, what did you learn that can help you move forward?

While you can't control the level of transparency others decide to disclose, understand what is best for *you* in the situation. What are the values driving your desire to be transparent in your communication (or not)? Think about the various outcomes based on different paths you could choose. Asking yourself the right questions can help guide you to the solutions that best fit the situation.

LESSON 5: SELF-LOVE AND TRUST

One of the most important things I learned about myself while going through my coach certification program was that, while I loved myself, I didn't love myself quite *enough* to always solve my own problems effectively. Once I became aware of it and shifted my perspective, I realized that many others struggle with exactly the same thing. I am a people pleaser by nature, always trying to make others feel safe and comfortable—sometimes at my own expense. I accept people for who they are, regardless of their decisions and actions. However, when it came to looking at myself, I was my absolute worst critic. I held myself to extremely high standards and constantly judged myself—something I would never do to anyone else!

Another thing I struggled with was feeling that, outside of my immediate family, I was the giver in most situations and that giving was rarely reciprocated. I silently wished others would take care of me the same way I took care of them. I occasionally found myself feeling lonely and resentful because I spent a lot of time building others up and feeling underappreciated in return. Because of this, I was extremely guarded in my relationships and only maintained close connections with people I completely trusted. I pushed away those I felt didn't truly value me and kept my inner circle extremely small to avoid spreading myself too thin emotionally. I was not great at small talk and generally avoided emotional connections with others.

I used to think caring for myself was selfish, and I didn't want to be viewed as selfish or conceited. But I knew I wanted to receive the same love I gave to others—I just didn't know how to make that happen. In one of my coach training sessions, I shared those feelings. I was starting to question some of my relationships that did not appear to be serving me well, but I was also afraid to let them go. This was primarily because I'd kept such long-term and close friendships that letting them go would feel like saying goodbye to a large part of myself.

One of my peers asked me to describe a friendship that made me very happy. I shared how I felt a mutual exchange of care and love with one particular friend, and it made me feel happy and inspired to give even more. You could feel the energy in the room shift to warmth and love. I was asked if I had more friends like that in my life, how things would be different. I responded, "It would obviously be amazing!"

Then, I was asked a question that rocked my world. "Apryl, if you took the care and love you give to others and directed even a little bit of it to yourself, what would change for you?" I had no idea how to respond and started to sob because I realized that I already knew exactly what I needed and wanted in order to feel loved. Why could I not give that to myself? Why was I so dependent on external validation to make me feel special? I left that training frustrated because I didn't know the answer.

Fast forward to a few months later when I had another conversation with a coaching peer who helped me realize that some deeply rooted experiences from my youth had led me down this path. I had always been held to a very high standard, and whenever I accomplished something great, it wasn't celebrated because it was *expected.* Subconsciously, I had allowed that experience to dim the light on my gifts I could share with the world. And what's even more interesting is that, as a result, I was constantly trying to help others realize how special they were when I didn't feel that way about myself.

I then realized I needed to start advocating for myself—to start looking in the mirror and celebrating all the things I have accomplished in my life, even the little things. I broke down my goals and threw myself a "party" every time I hit a new milestone. I acknowledged that my journey is my *own,* and I am always exactly where I need to be. I worked to accept that while I can never make everyone happy, I *can* make myself happy.

Self-love can be really tough to master. It's always a work in progress, but it's important to note that you *are* good enough. And you absolutely 100 percent deserve all the love in this world. My best advice is to surround yourself with a loving community, and be willing to be vulnerable and ask for what you want and need. When you need a pick-me-up, ask yourself what you are proud of. If you're feeling down, ask someone to share some words of inspiration. And if you don't know who to contact, I am here to help shine that light for you.

COMMUNICATION

Looking at all the different types of relationships that exist in one's life, there is one main key to all healthy relationships: *communication*. Without the ability to communicate well, we are often left to confusion, drama, and potential damage to the relationship, whether with others or even yourself. When communication is strong, the opportunities for growth and love increase.

My journey to becoming a life coach has transformed the way I look at relationships. I realized that the relationships in my life were an opportunity to help me gain awareness about who I truly am and what I believe. When I admire someone, it gives me a new perspective on the values that are important to me. At the same time, when someone challenges me in a negative manner, I can again see which values are not being honored. Instead of becoming angry and frustrated, I now look at any situation as an opportunity for growth.

As you become more aware of how you react to various situations, assess how it makes you feel. Be willing to have these difficult conversations with those around you—and, most importantly, yourself. When you align yourself with what you really want, you will find much more peace and joy in life, and all the other stresses will melt away.

seven

PERSONAL DEVELOPMENT

$\mathcal{Looking}$ back at the thirty-year-old version of myself, I giggle at the thought that I had absolutely no clue what "personal development" meant. Back then, the only type of development I knew about was professional development, which was primarily focused on one's career path. But growth in the other areas of my life didn't seem to exist. The only concept of "working on myself" revolved around therapy and counseling which, for a long time, in my world had the stigma of something being "wrong" that needed to be fixed.

What I didn't realize was my life has actually been one long personal-development journey, and indeed there was never anything "wrong" with me. I didn't arrive at this realization until after I was able to release some of those negative thoughts that had been holding me back for many years, while in therapy, and even more during the process of becoming a coach. But once I became more aware, I learned how to be intentional about developing into the person I ultimately wanted to be, rather than letting life just unfold on its own. For so many years, I'd let the world define what success meant for me: study hard in school and go to a good college, obtain a degree to get a well-paying job, and afford to pay for all the things that I wanted. Then meet a man who made me happy, have kids, and live in a nice-sized suburban home. Once I'd checked off all of those boxes, I said, "And now what?" Something was still missing. And that started me on the path to seek the answers.

In this chapter, I share some the lessons I've learned about myself along my journey of personal development and the specific process I followed to align my reality with my true passions.

CREATING YOUR PERSONAL DEVELOPMENT JOURNEY

Step 1: Self-Awareness

Self-awareness is the first step to initiating change—whether simple or substantial—in your life. An easy example is when you're feeling hungry. When you realize it, your body reacts and tells you to eat some food. Similarly, this example holds true for when I lost a big chunk of my hair. I was completely oblivious to the amount of stress I was putting upon myself, so my body decided to send me a signal. Once I was aware of this signal, I knew it was time to make some adjustments in my life.

Awareness is what allows you to reflect on where you are and decide whether you want to embrace those qualities or make modifications. As I finally started to pay attention to my actions, traits, and feelings, I gained much more clarity about myself and the best ways to move forward.

Step 2: Identifying What You Want

Once you know something needs to change, or even stay the same, it's time to set an intention. For instance, "I'm tired of feeling unfulfilled and want to focus on what makes me happy!" This is what I told myself shortly before I left my last job. And once you set an intention, you need to problem solve what that would actually look like in a clear way.

Apryl's Tips

In my search for personal fulfillment, I took the time to explore what I already knew by asking many questions, including:

- What are the most important things to me?
- What are my top three values?
- What makes me happy?
- What activities do I enjoy?
- What am I passionate about?
- What do I wish I had more of in my life?
- *Why* do I want these things in my life?

Next, I envisioned myself one year from now—which was far enough away to give me time to create a more fulfilling life, yet close enough to set realistic goals. I wrote a few sentences about what my life would look like in a year, using the present tense, such as, but not limited to:

- My career: I am helping people decrease the stress in their lives as they complete the many tasks on their plate, so they can enjoy life to the fullest.

- Who I am spending time with: I spend most of my time with family and close friends, and I'm meeting new and exciting people who help me grow my business.

- Travel: I'm going to Hawaii, Michigan, New York, California, Florida, and Puerto Rico—some for business, some for family vacations.

- Family time: We travel as a family every few months, including ski and beach vacations, and I'm spending quality time with our extended family.

- My income: I have created a business that has replaced the income I earned in my previous job, and my family will maintain (or increase) our net worth despite my change in careers.

- My level of fun: On a scale of one to ten, I've raised the level of fun in my life from a six to an eight or higher.

- The impact I have made on the world: I am infusing more positivity into those I interact with by sharing my story and experiences and helping them live their own fulfilling lives.

- Where I live: I am living in Chicago, but have a more open mind to move if the right opportunity arises.

- How I feel about life on a daily basis: I'm busy, but not nearly as stressed as I was a year ago. The things that fill my time are of my choosing, and I don't feel as if I'm wasting time or going through the motions, and I'm having a ton of fun!

All of those statements helped me paint a picture of what I wanted my life to look like after twelve months. The next step was to identify *how* to make it happen. Remember, you can ask yourself exactly the same questions (or different ones) that I did and make the same positive intentions for your own life.

Step 3: What's Getting in the Way?
In order to make some changes in life, some things have to give. It's important to use time-management and productivity tools to create space for what we want to accomplish. The modifications I like to make get rid of what I call "time suckers." These are the things that drain your energy, piss you off, take too long to do, and/or don't add value to your life. In essence, the things that stress you out.

I have worked with many of my clients to tame or completely eliminate their various time suckers: Netflix addictions, long commutes, toxic friendships, unmanageable e-mail inboxes, poor sleeping habits, social media compulsions, and the list goes on and on. With my clients, I spend time to fully understand the reasons behind each activity's presence in their lives; then we come to an understanding of how to adjust their relationship with that activity to free up time for the lives they truly want.

In some cases, we choose a more productive relationship with those time suckers, and for others, we let them go.

Other types of time suckers can be a bit harder to eliminate. Sometimes the perceptions, beliefs, and attitudes that have become part of your wiring may actually be preventing you from moving forward. Because of that, it's important to understand how your own perspectives and beliefs are affecting you. Do you ever ask yourself why others might find completing a certain task easy, or how others might be completely fearless in something that scares the living crap out of you? Or how some people are afraid of or angry about things you feel are trivial? This is because at some point in your life, you may have experienced something that created a filter to keep you safe and not reignite any painful or uncomfortable thoughts. Everyone has different experiences that create different filters. These filters show up in a few different ways:

- Limiting beliefs: This term explains itself—a belief you have about yourself, your life, or the world that limits you in some way. For example, I used to think I could never be an author. Or, I remember saying, "I am not smart enough to be in a high-level position in a company." Looks like I proved them both wrong! If you catch yourself stating a limiting belief (or if you catch someone else making that statement), ask, "How true is that belief?" Taking this a step further, list all the factual evidence that supports your response to that question and share it with someone you can trust to get an outsider's perspective. Sometimes we have such strong-rooted beliefs that we may not even realize how limiting they are. A differentiating factor for a limiting belief is when you "settle" for not having or doing something you strongly desire for yourself. For example, if you say, "I'm a parent now, and I just can't have fun like I used to," there would be great value in examining it as a potential limiting belief.

- Assumptions: These are statements based on historical occurrences. In other words, because something happened one way multiple times in the past, it will always happen the same way. Perhaps a person assumes he or she will never settle down or get married after one-too-many failed relationships. Or assuming you will never drop the pounds after multiple diets produced no results. When you find yourself making assumptions, ask, "Just because it's happened before, why does it need to happen that way again?"

- Interpretations: These statements occur when others create a judgment or opinion *they* believe to be true, whether or not the statement is factually accurate. What comes to mind are optical illusions, such as that famous dress on the Internet that some saw as blue and black, but others swore it was white and gold. Or when you read a text message from a friend without an exclamation point at the end, you interpret that they are angry at you. Before you make any interpretive claims, ask yourself, "What's another way to look at that?"

- The "inner critic": That voice only inside *your* mind that says you're not good enough. This is one of the most powerful filters I have built up over time: I don't deserve good things; I'm a fraud; I'm not important; or I'm not smart. And, man, that inner critic held me back from so many things. Of the four types of filters, the inner critic is the most difficult one to overcome, as it often relates to deeply rooted, painful experiences from your youth. In these cases, the first question to ask is, "What real evidence do I have that I'm not good enough for _____ (fill in the blank)?" The answers will likely bring up some assumptions, limiting beliefs, or interpretations that you've created for yourself.

Getting past some of the deeper-rooted time suckers requires a bit of self-love and care to rewire and untangle those limiting feelings and move forward. When I quit my last job, I spent several months in therapy trying to navigate my thoughts and feelings. I had so many limiting beliefs about myself and was stuck feeling unloved and believing that I needed money in order to be "successful." I was always aspiring to higher-level, higher-paying jobs, and when that didn't happen, I felt that I wasn't smart enough to be in those positions.

Therapy was fantastic for me because it helped me identify the unhealthy, deep-rooted beliefs that had been holding me *back* for so long and let me move *forward*. I remember telling my therapist in my last session that I was interested in becoming a coach. She reminded me that I really needed to "get real" with myself and be in a good place in my own mind to be able help others. With her help, I knew I was on the right path, but she was totally right because the process of becoming a life coach was an emotionally long and hard road. That said, I'm even better equipped to help others because I did my own heavy lifting and reframed how I look at life.

Step 4: Creating and Executing a New Plan of Action
After wading through the weeds of your current life, this step is where your new life starts to take shape. You have your one-year vision, but might not know the path yet. To better illuminate this path, I use the process of reverse planning. First, ask yourself what would need to be in place at the six-month mark in order to reach your year-end goal? For example, if I wanted to start a new job I love in one year, I might consider being ready to actively look for jobs by that time. In order to do that, I would need to have my résumé ready, know what kind of jobs I wanted to apply for, and narrow down my location search, to name a few.

Then, I need to consider what should happen by the three-month mark in order to accomplish the six-month goals? I should be updating my résumé, starting to network, and speaking with mentors. Next, plan backward even further to create the one-month goals. What would I need to be working on in order to be on target with my three-month goals? Perhaps I will need to decide who my mentors are, commit to attending networking events, and decide if I want to stay in the same industry or move to a new one.

And finally, identify the best actions to take within that first week to accomplish your one-month goals. In this case, I might consider researching available jobs in the area, reflect on what I like about my current job and what I might desire in my next role, research some career guides online, and identify methods of getting support in this decision. I might also ask myself *why* I want a new job one year from now. From there, I would take action on those items, making observations along the way. At the end of the week, reflect on what was accomplished, and set new goals for the following week, making sure the plans are still in alignment or making modifications as needed and continuing to push forward.

One of the key steps in the reverse-planning process is constant reflection. So many things can happen in the course of a year, including the creation of new time suckers and unexpected events happening. It's not necessary to know the entire plan in a step-by-step manner, but do have some guidelines that can keep you on track. It's also important to know that plans are always subject to change. Perhaps during the new job search, an opportunity for a promotion falls upon your lap. And maybe you decide to take it! The good news is that you can revisit new goals for yourself at that point and keep moving forward.

I have been following this process throughout my personal development journey in recent years, and it's been the main reason I'm getting so much done. Being able to understand my vision of the road ahead has kept me focused, even when new ideas popped into my head. And to be cautious of overcommitment, I consciously stored my great ideas in a safe place for when I was ready to take action on them.

THE CHEERFUL MIND JOURNEY

On my long personal journey to The Cheerful Mind, I've learned much about myself and life—some things I didn't realize until they were pointed out to me, and others I knew but didn't know how to tackle. As you read the following, think about how these issues and characteristics might relate (or not) to your own situation to kick-start the search for your own cheerful mind!

PERFECTIONISM

One of my mentors referred to himself as a "recovering perfectionist" during a lunch conversation about my career aspirations. At the time, I thought to myself, *I want to be one of those!* I knew that my tendency toward perfectionism was preventing me from accomplishing my ultimate goal, which was to love my life and be happy. I was extremely afraid of failing and of people judging me harshly if I made mistakes. It caused unnecessary stress in my life. In addition, as I was growing up, I was always expected to perform well. So despite my many accomplishments, I often felt they weren't good enough, leading me to push myself even harder.

The process of becoming a "recovering perfectionist" meant looking at and defining "failure" differently. The following new points of view are how I turned failure into something more fun:

1. Failure makes you stronger: When you fail, you are learning what doesn't work, and it gets you one step closer to knowing what does. The ability to collect more data points in your trial and error allows you

to gain a more substantial perspective about how to achieve success and even replicate it.

2. Making mistakes lets you appreciate your successes even more: When trying to accomplish something, if you succeed relatively quickly, you can sometimes forget the greatness of your accomplishment and may take it for granted. When you work hard for a goal and finally accomplish it, the victory is sweeter and more meaningful.

3. Failure can make for interesting stories: While it is cool to hear a success story about accomplishing something, think about the fun and interesting stories that can arise from a failure. Think about entertaining epic-fail videos or inspiring videos about a failure that leads to bigger and better things for the person. The journey is JUST as important as the end goal!

SPIRITUALITY

The topic of spirituality has always been a touchy one for me, and I equated religion with spirituality, as many people do. I was raised Catholic and lived in a primarily Jewish community, so as I grew older, I had many questions about religion. If someone had different religious beliefs than me, what did that mean? I wasn't quite sure. And did I believe 100 percent of everything I heard in my own church? Could I not practice that religion if I wasn't completely committed? I didn't have the answers.

For many years, I was terrified to vocalize my feelings and concerns because I was surrounded by so many different viewpoints, including some very strong opinions. I also feared what might happen if people/my family knew I wasn't sure I believed what they did, so I spent a lot of time avoiding the topic.

Fast forward to more recent times when I married someone raised in the Lutheran faith, and even though we were both Christian, the denominations had some differing beliefs and practices. I knew this would become a more important issue to resolve as we raised our children.

When attending my coach certification training, I noticed that "Spirituality" was one of the pieces of the Wheel of Life, and this concerned me. I wasn't sure what I believed—if anything. Was I not spiritual if I questioned religion? I knew others who regularly practiced meditation and considered themselves spiritual, but I didn't do that either. Was this the area of my life that was completely lacking? I spent quite some time seeking the answers.

My first step was to identify exactly what spirituality meant for *me*. So I decided to speak with many different types of people to get a better understanding of what spirituality meant for them and, somewhat to my surprise, I heard a wide variety of answers and noticed the trend that spirituality is based on each individual's belief system.

As a result, I could look at religion as communities of people who simply shared the same beliefs. So I needed to start clarifying my beliefs (at least for myself) in order to move forward and work toward resolving this issue. I jotted down some notes:

- I believe that everyone in this world deserves an amazing, happy life.

- I believe that almost all people have good intentions and don't automatically default to conflict and evil.

- I believe that anyone who has done wrong is not forever destined to be evil; they have opportunities to change.

- I believe that negativity in the world is a result of a chain reaction of misinterpretations and assumptions.

- I believe in science and what it has proven to be factual based on research and experimentation, but I am also open to the possibility that anything "discovered" to date can still be proven wrong as society advances.

- I believe there is a possibility there may be other forms of life in the universe.

- I believe our spirit does not die with our bodies, but I'm not sure what happens in the afterlife.

- I used to believe in fate, but after lengthy discussions with my husband on the topic, I'm not so sure. I don't believe some higher being is deciding what occurs in and around my life; rather, my life is impacted by a combination of various decisions made by me and others, science, and an element of chance.

- Beliefs can be changed at any point in time based on new information or experiences. They are not set in stone.

These were the first things that came to mind as I declared my beliefs, and simply vocalizing them created so much more peace in my life. As a result, I realized why spirituality is an important component of the wheel of life. The confidence of owning what I believed brought a sense of joy to my life, and in times of stress I could come back to that same place.

I am not saying that my beliefs will be the same five years from now, one year from now, or even six months from now. As I gain more information and perspective, I have the power to change my beliefs. And I respectfully accept—and am open to hearing—other people's beliefs, whether or not they align with mine. We are each entitled to our own opinions, and it is quite possible that others' perspectives may help to shape our own. I can embrace my Christian upbringing, but reserve the right to my own interpretation of it. And with that said, I now live my true, authentic, and spiritual self, unfiltered by others' judgments, and can just be me.

OVERCOMMITMENT AND/OR OVERGIVING

One of the reasons I like to coach people who resonate with the word "overcommitted" is because I have historically been my toughest client in this area. There are three components to overcommitment that I have been actively trying to improve while on my personal development journey.

First, because I am easily inspired and am also good at taking action (whereas some people are rarely inspired and take little action), my plate gets very full, very fast. Second, I love being generous, so I'm really good at saying *yes* and not so good at saying *no*. Third, I don't generally like to ask for help, partly because I enjoy a challenge and solving problems, but when the problem is one that I can't solve alone, I tend to not lean on others because I'm sure they are busy with their own issues. These qualities turned me into an overcommitted person, which led to me feeling resentful and overwhelmed and frequently sent me to the verge of burnout.

I have to constantly push outside my comfort zone to say *yes* only to the things that are in line with my values. I have to ask for help to get more things done, and I have to visualize my limits. I greatly depend on my calendar and to-do list and keep a repository of my wild ideas in what I call my "think tank." My calendar helps me exercise saying *no* when necessary. As a result, I still remain busy, but I feel more in control of my life.

LEVERAGING THE LAW OF ATTRACTION

I'm the type of person who doesn't automatically believe in theories, laws, and research studies until I experience concrete evidence in my own life that they are true—or at least true for me. Many times, I have experienced a so-called law or theory and realized it only after the fact. The Law of Attraction is a phenomenon I experienced later in life. As I mentioned in an earlier chapter, the Law of Attraction states that "like energy attracts like energy." You can apply this principle to many different areas of life, and here I apply it to positive thinking. Combining a positive mindset with the Law of Attraction and understanding the infectious nature of positivity dramatically changed my perspective about how I wanted to live.

I frequently viewed life as one big set of problems to overcome so, of course, problems continued to surround me. My default was assuming that most people were trying to take advantage of me, and I feared trusting others. Some of this was due to past experiences and my observations. I avoided making eye contact with people because I worried about sending incorrect signals, and I rarely gave my opinions and perspectives because they felt uncomfortable to me.

As a result, I placed an invisible shield to guard me, which I later realized only served to prevent me from being my happiest self. I shifted to a more positive mindset and became more trusting, rather than fearing society was plotting against me. Even trying to look someone in the eye with a smile dramatically changed my world. People started smiling back (and it wasn't creepy!), and what I experienced over time was increased positivity. My "problems" became opportunities for something new and different.

These new experiences led me to consider how I could more actively turn negative events in my life into positive ones. I began analyzing my negative interpretations and replacing them with more positive ones. For example, I once had a trapeze performance scheduled, but felt I had nothing exciting to showcase because I hadn't made enough "progress" in my classes—even though I had studied flying trapeze for more than two years and had achieved the level in which some might start considering doing it as a career. I almost missed the show because I only wanted to share something that would WOW the crowd. Instead, I decided to focus on just having fun, which was why I started doing flying trapeze in the first place. Of course, one of the trapeze tricks didn't catch and, instead of beating myself up over looking like a fool, I acknowledged the trick as one of the more advanced and appreciated that I had the skill to even attempt it. One of my friends even commented that it showed that I was human!

When I began to shift my perspective, stress and anxiety began to dissipate. Some of the things I had previously thought of as the "end of the world' (for instance, finding a typo in an important e-mail had created so much anxiety for me!) were not as painful as I'd thought they might be. I would ask myself, "What is a *worse* thing that could have happened?" I had to *train* my brain to think more about the fact that a mistake wasn't a challenge—but rather an opportunity.

Another life-coaching principle, "Pain is inevitable; suffering is optional," struck a chord with me because, of course, we can't be happy 100 percent of the time. There will be pain, and there will be sadness. But, really, as we navigate through our pain, is it going to help to suffer as well? I used to complain a lot more than I do now: "Ugh, I have so much work to do." "Ugh, I'm so tired." "Ugh, why is she so obnoxious?" When I was able to shift my thinking away from placing blame on other people or things, I became more productive and peaceful. When I find myself in a complaining mode, I ask myself the big question, *SO WHAT? Is living with negativity and stress worth being a victim to these thoughts?*

BEING A MULTIPOTENTIALITE
On one of my very first podcast interviews, the host introduced me as a "multipotentialite." I wasn't quite sure what that meant, but I knew I needed to learn more about it and meet others who identified as one. Emilie Wapnick's TEDx talk clarified it: "A multipotentialite is someone with multiple interests and creative pursuits." She called out the pattern of dabbling in various projects and activities and

feeling anxiety about the inability to focus on just one thing. She used the big example of answering the question, "What do you want to be when you grow up?"

As soon as I heard this, I thought, *That's me!* I had always felt like something was wrong with the fact that I kept switching careers. I loved the challenge of trying new things, but found myself almost bored once I settled into a routine, which, looking back now, I understand why I was ready to change jobs every few years. I also have a multitude of interests: I loved music, but I also loved sports. I sometimes feel like a tomboy, but can also feel very feminine. I am a math and science nerd, but also aspired to be an author. I felt like I was pretty good at a number of things, but was an expert at none. During my coaching-certification training, the word I used to describe myself was "versatile." And it was only at that point, at the age of thirty-five, when I embraced that part of myself. Who knew there was a term to describe what I'd been experiencing my entire life?

Emilie Wapnick mentions the three "superpowers" of multipotentialites in her talk: adaptability, idea synthesis, and rapid learning. Each of those superpowers completely resonated with me. I already mentioned my versatile nature, but I also adopted new skills relatively quickly, and loved taking experiences from one of my many interests and applying them to another.

What's interesting about this new way of describing myself is that for much of my life, I'd felt fairly isolated—as if most people outside my small inner circle of friends and family didn't really understand me. I had so many different interests, but most people could relate to only one area of my life and not the others. I felt like an oddball of sorts, and that I didn't "fit in."

Learning that I'm a multipotentialite allowed me to realize two things. I should embrace the versatility in all aspects of my life. Perhaps how I work with clients will differ in a few years. Maybe I will hang up my flying-trapeze belt someday and try something else new. But change is not an indicator of failure or lack of focus—rather, I'm tapping into unchartered territory I am excited to tackle.

Second, I realized no one is better than anyone else; they're just different. If you have ever felt like you didn't fit in, you're not alone. Keep searching and being your true, authentic self, and you WILL find your people. Embrace your quirks, and live your life your way.

OUTWARD PROCESSING

When I was young, I used to hate raising my hand in class to speak because I found it hard to come up with clear and concise answers on the spot. I feared what would happen if I gave a wrong answer. It made me feel like I wasn't smart, even though I knew I was; I had very good grades to prove my intelligence. Yet, I also knew that I had to invest more time into studying than some of my peers, and I was a bit ashamed that I didn't grasp some concepts as quickly. I was also frequently teased for taking too long to get to the point of any story I told. This trait impacted my ability to have comfortable, impromptu, quick conversations with people. I thrived in deep, one-on-one conversations and clammed up in larger groups.

During my first coach-training weekend, those suppressed feelings rose to the surface. I had completed all of the advance homework before my training started and walked into the room feeling pretty confident about what I had learned. But after a few hours, I was again afraid to raise my hand. After observing others' responses, I noticed that I would have responded differently and questioned whether I'd understood the material correctly. I grew silent.

On the third day of training, I walked into the classroom overwhelmed with excitement and wanted to share an amazing story from the night before as I was reconnected with an old friend. I started to tell the story and, as I expected, it took some time for me to get to the point. The instructor finally asked me to cut my story down and get to the point, and inside I was *crushed*. I grew silent. I actually felt tears welling up inside me (I was functioning on very little sleep and had been emotional throughout the training).

During a break, I approached my trainer and told him I was feeling bad. When he asked me to explain exactly how I was feeling, I couldn't find the words. As he continued to dig to help me explain what I was feeling about him, I reluctantly muttered something to the effect of, "I felt you were being an a**hole." Tears started streaming down my face. My trainer looked at me with compassion and thanked me for sharing. I started crying more. He said, "It's okay. You like to process outwardly, and that is completely normal. Many people do this."

As soon as he said this, a light turned on in my brain. *Wait, there is such a thing? I'm not weird?* I started combing through my memories of similar situations and began looking at the situation from a different perspective. Maybe this was just a part of my personality. Do I like this about myself? If I could change this about myself, would I? What should I do with this new information now?

A few days later, I came to the decision that I wanted to embrace this part of me. I decided to lovingly warn people ahead of time of a potentially lengthy story, and it gave us some additional laughs. I even realized that one of my close friends was an outward processor, too (no *wonder* we got along so well!), and we would always wrap up our stories by saying, "Long story *long,*" instead of "Long story short." I felt more comfortable knowing that I didn't have to raise my hand in a classroom setting if I didn't want to, and it had no impact on my intelligence.

A month after my coach training, while trying to define the messaging for my new business, I decided that since I am an outward processor, I should just write a book. A book would be a helpful way for me to process my thoughts, while also providing those who wanted to understand what I do with something tangible. Great way of multitasking, don't you think?

SELF-CONFIDENCE

Confidence is such an important factor in your ability to be successful, regardless of how you define it. After seeing how much I've learned about myself in this process, the common theme is related to my level of self-confidence. My earlier lack of confidence had directly affected my happiness.

As a perfectionist, I did not have the self-confidence to trust that a "flawed" outcome could still be the right outcome. With spirituality, I wasn't confident enough to own my beliefs. As an overgiver, I lacked the confidence to know that my contributions to others were "good enough." Before I learned about multipotentialites, I thought something was wrong with me, and I didn't have the self-confidence to embrace my unique qualities.

After being with my husband for over fourteen years, we had a discussion one day about how much my confidence has changed since he met me. Even though I am relatively outgoing now, I was a shy nineteen-year-old when we first met. I used to think he was significantly more intelligent than me because he was quicker to learn things and better at seeing the "big picture." He was wildly confident about his statements, even if a claim wasn't completely accurate.

On the other hand, I needed a little more time to process; I was extremely detail oriented and would never make any claims unless 100 percent sure my answer was correct. But now, I feel we are on parallel ground, and the only thing that's changed is my level of self-confidence.

I believe the reason my husband is naturally self-confident is that he accepts himself as he *is* and doesn't let any failure define his worth. He's willing to push the envelope and stand up for whatever he believes in, even if it's against the status quo. He believes that every problem can be solved, and I absolutely admire that about him. Of course, he, like everyone, has some insecurities and fears, but he's willing to look beyond them and trust that everything is right where it needs to be.

And now that I've finally learned the same things for myself, my self-confidence has increased, as well. While I still occasionally struggle in certain situations, I'm much more willing to take a step into the fire and at least try something different. Committing to my personal development has changed my life, and I can't wait to see what lies ahead.

If there's anything I can recommend to you as you're reading this book, please consider investing in your own personal growth. Whether or not you choose me to be your "personal cheerleader," just know that life after personal development is so sweet. And if a healthy work-life balance is what you seek, or even the accomplishment of any important goal, I firmly believe that making your own journey to a cheerful mind will significantly impact your happiness and success.

eight

MY JOURNEY TO THE CHEERFUL MIND

When I look back on my life these days, I reflect on the many different journeys I've already taken and how grateful I am for my experiences. I'm thankful that my parents were ambitious and instilled that same spirit in me at a young age. I'm thankful that I've met so many wonderful people with different perspectives, who have helped me craft my own. I'm grateful for my body that sent me the appropriate signals and gave me the opportunity to make incredible changes in my life. And I am proud that instead of allowing myself to settle for mediocrity, I broke through my fears in search of what my heart was craving: a more cheerful mind.

One of my biggest hurdles was to understand the true meaning of success. What I know now is that there is no one definition. Detaching from the pressure society dictates about being "successful" has catalyzed a new life for me, one in which *I* defined a successful life on my own terms. While it's great to receive input and opinions from family, friends, and mentors, ultimately the lives we create for ourselves are completely ours to choose. As a result of this journey, I now choose to first follow what I believe is best for *me*, instead of putting everyone else before me. And if it means I "go against the grain" sometimes, then so be it.

My journey hasn't been easy. A lot of emotions arose when I challenged my previous beliefs and perspectives and redefined what is truly important with more clarity. I've been challenged to my core and had to make many tough decisions about my deep-rooted beliefs; some of my beliefs remain, while I let others go. My friendships and relationships have evolved and changed, some for the better, while others have drifted. I still come up against fear, and at times the old version of me resurfaces. I fall off the wagon and have to work hard to jump back on. But I don't *ever* give up, and I can't put a price on how much happier I feel in my own skin these days—and others can definitely see the difference.

I think about how much more positive my life is now: On a recent trip to Hawaii, my entire suitcase burst open on the runway, due to a broken zipper, with all of my clothes falling out. As I stood there, hungry and tired after a long flight, with my two young kids running around the airport like wild animals, I started laughing. The first thing that came out of my mouth was, "Well, I guess that means we get to buy a new suitcase!"

The old version of me would have been huffing and

puffing, frustrated and eager to get back to the hotel to do a full accounting of my wardrobe, and feeling our vacation was going to continue to be a disaster. (Yes, I admit I was an OCD drama queen! So embarrassing.) My new reaction shocked even my husband, who has known me for over a decade and knew this wasn't my typical response. That is just one example of how being intentional about personal development and becoming a professional coach has dramatically changed my life.

During my life coach training, I realized how much I had been trying to "coach" myself over the years without even knowing it. While I have generally been a self-sufficient "doer," once a peer was assigned to coach me for a few months, I was shocked by the amount of incremental progress I made over doing things on my own. I felt like I was on fire, working at a productive pace I had never experienced before. I was held accountable by a professional who helped me process my thoughts, rather than spin in circles when I became stuck. Having a coach on my side allowed me to achieve my desired results faster and has been absolutely worth the investment to regain my precious time. Because of coaching, I now have more time to enjoy my family, travel every few months, and maintain a healthier lifestyle—all while being financially stable, loving my career, connecting with friends, and having the confidence and comfort in knowing the path I am on is the perfect one for me. I consistently integrate my work-life balance tips into my own life:

- I know that "balance" is always evolving.
- I continue to stay self-aware.

- I constantly align my life with my values.

- I prioritize and plan, but allow for flexibility.

- I set boundaries for myself and slow down when I need to.

- I make commitments, but also keep an open mind.

- I do my best to interweave the different areas of my life and multitask to accomplish more with less effort.

HOW THE CHEERFUL MIND, INC., CAN HELP YOU
What Is a Professional Coach?

There are many different coaches out there with different styles and strategies. Before I share how my coaching differs from others, let me first start by clarifying what a coach does:

- Coaches have no agenda other than helping clients get what they want in life. There are times when a coach may act as a *consultant*, suggesting ideas from his/her knowledge and experience, but, primarily, a coach partners and works with the client to implement an effective action plan.

- A coach differs from a *mentor* in the sense that a coach does not use his/her personal experiences as a model of success for the client; rather, the coach is an expert on the coaching process and focuses on letting clients be the experts of their own lives.

- Coaching is not the same as *therapy*; a therapist's typical function is to help clients fix problems and overcome issues (focusing more on "why"), while coaches focus on solutions that help the client move forward (focusing more on "how").

- Professional coaches do not operate like *sports coaches*—although similar, professional coaching is focused on bringing out the best in the client, not in competition or a win/lose scenario.

- Finally, the difference between a coach and a *friend* is that a coach focuses on being nonjudgmental and objective, and holds the client accountable for the goals he/she wants to achieve. Friends tend to give you advice based on their knowledge of you, and may not point out various issues you should be addressing for fear of hurting your feelings.

Coaching is a confidential and safe environment that takes you from where you currently are to where you want to be, in an efficient manner. It is a collaborative effort that is solely based on the client's agenda. When you work with a coach, you're investing in *yourself*, not the coach!

Apryl's Coaching Style

If you haven't figured out my style yet from everything you've read so far, let me summarize what you can expect from me:

- Laid back: I absolutely enjoy infusing humor and fun into my coaching any chance I have.

- Efficient and organized: My expertise in process efficiency is a result of being able to fully understand the details and creating the best options based on a particular situation.

- Adaptable: I'm the type of coach that can kick your butt when you need it and challenge you in the right way; however, I am also compassionate and empathetic to your needs and can help you back to taking action. I believe that in coaching there's no one-size-fits-all model to getting things done, so I adapt to your preferred learning styles.

- Versatile: I've been through many different experiences in my life, which gives me a multitude of perspectives to pull from at any given time. I have an analytical brain by nature, but I can leverage it to be creative.

- Determined: I focus on making things happen. Your success is my success. I will leverage every resource I have and use it to help you win.

- Energetic: I cheered on sports teams from the sidelines for over ten years. I will celebrate every victory with you, be encouraging when things get tough, and always be supportive of you no matter what.

- Honesty: I will always share my honest observations with you and approach you without judgment—only curiosity.

- Analytical: I combine my background in engineering and teaching and apply it to life and happiness, or as some of my friends have noted, I do "engineering of the mind." I utilize my problem-solving skills to ask you the right guiding questions that will lead to the answers you are seeking for yourself.

Creating the Roadmap to Your Success

Many people I work with have two main struggles:

- The first is that they have big goals and dreams to accomplish, but they don't know how to create an action plan to turn them into reality.

- Second, they feel "stuck," either when trying to get started or they hit one (or more) roadblocks somewhere along the way.

I walk my clients through the following process to accomplish the change they want in their lives, something I like to call their "strategic life plan":

Step 1: Identify the Vision – In this step, I gain a clear understanding of what the client wants to create for himself.

Step 2: Assess the Current State – During this stage, we dive in and look at what is currently working well and what areas need improvement. We examine priorities and values and create a baseline from which to begin our work.

Step 3: Brainstorm – This is when we start investigating new ideas. Most of the research is done in this phase, and we consider different ways to address the issues at hand.

Step 4: Create the Action Plan – After research, we create an action plan. I like to execute this is by reverse planning: setting a goal in a specific timeline, moving from the end-goal backward to the present, and asking what specifically needs to be accomplished at each milestone.

Step 5: Monitor – In this step, the action plan goes into full execution mode. We make observations to determine what is working well and what isn't.

Step 6: Reflect and Reset – This step takes the observations from the Monitoring phase and allows for modifications to the action plan as needed. Although this is the final step, the process doesn't end here. Steps 4 through 6 are repeated as often as necessary, and at times, we may introduce new ideas and begin again at Step 1. I walk my clients through this process as we work toward introducing the changes they desire in their lives.

If you are ready for significant change in your life and want your own cheerful mind, but don't know where to start; or if you've been trying to make things happen, but are tired of going it alone; or if you're spinning in your own self-doubt that real change and absolute fulfillment can happen for you, I invite you to hop on the phone with me and chat. I'd love to help you in any way I can.

You can reach out to me here:

http://www.thecheerfulmind.com/

and during our call, I will assess your situation and give you a kick-start in the right direction...and if you desire to work with me further, that would be icing on the cake!

What Does Success Mean to Me?

In my journey to redefine success, ultimately I found that success means I love my life and everything in it. I believe success should feel effortless, and working too hard and/ or stressing too much is *not* success for me. I don't need to be wealthy at the cost of being able to live my life the way I want. I don't need a high-powered job that keeps me working one-hundred-hour weeks and leaves me with no time for my family or friends.

The most important thing I've learned is that I can redefine success *anytime* I want. There's no one definition. And nobody needs to approve of it other than me.

How Do You Find Success in Balance?
I challenge you to ask yourself in your journey of finding balance, "What do *you* need to feel balanced? How would you feel when your life is in balance?" Without knowing the answers to these questions, you'll never get there. But you *can* get there.

Many people say that you can't have everything. And to some extent, that is true; we all have a limited amount of time on this earth, and we have to prioritize how to spend it. However, I firmly believe that it *is* possible to have everything you truly want in life. It might require some problem solving and the willingness to commit to try things that may succeed or fail, but you need to know that *anything* is possible. Sure, you may see studies that display general trends, but those statistics don't define your own personal capacity. You *can* create the life you want; you just have to believe in yourself and have the right motivation to make it a reality. And I believe in you.

FINAL THOUGHTS

Here we are, at the end of the book. Thanks so much for reading! But now, you're probably thinking, "what's next?"

Well, this obviously isn't the end of the road! Are you feeling inspired to take the journey to your cheerful mind, too, and ready to take some action right now?

If yes, hop on over to
    http://www.findingsuccessinbalance.com/nextsteps
for a special gift from me. Let's have more fun and get stuff done together!

To your success,

ACKNOWLEDGMENTS

I could go on and on about the people who have impacted my life in so many different ways, but I must first thank my parents, Tony and Eleanor Zarate, who dedicated their lives to ensure that I had the best life possible. Mom and Dad, I hope you realize that this book is the product of all *your* hard work. I love you immensely and hope I've made you proud over the years!

To my brother, Andrew Zarate, who has been my rock since we stopped fighting and became allies in 1993 (haha!). Drew, thanks for giving me unconditional love and being my protector every step of the way. I am your number one fan, and I look forward to expanding our legacy with you and Mona at our side.

Thanks to Danielle Schaefer, who helped me survive the early years of parenting and whose dedication and care for me and my sons has been amazing. You are one of the main reasons I can do all the things I do. Love you, girl!

To my editor and writing coach, Jill Welsh, who helped me tame my energetic exclamation points and held my hand through writing my first book ever, amid all of the delays of life. Thank you, Jill, for having faith in me, being the *only* other set of eyes during the writing process, and helping boost my confidence whenever I needed it!

To my team who helped me take this manuscript from a Microsoft Word document sitting on my computer to a book visible to the universe (Kim Bookless, Bethany Brown and the Cadence Group, Gwyn Snider of GKS Creative, Barbara

Hague, and Sarah Gilbert and the Smith Publicity team), I would have been overcommitted trying to do all of this on my own without you! Thank you for your support in making the publishing experience a fun one!

I'd like to thank the Institute for Professional Excellence in Coaching (IPEC) and my fellow classmates for completely transforming my life and challenging me to realize my true potential so that I could share it with the world. So much of what I've written here is a result of what I learned during this program.

To Paul Corona for being the first person to ask me the *one* question that changed the trajectory of my life forever. I don't think you realize how much you've impacted my life. Thank you *so* much!

To everyone who has been a part of my super-intimate inner circle and already knows many of the stories I shared in this book (you know who you are!), thank you for cheering on this cheerleader. Mad love to you all.

To my AMAZING clients: you never cease to inspire me, and I'm absolutely honored to know that, out of all life coaches out there, you've entrusted me to help you shine your light on the world and make our universe that much brighter.

And finally, to the one constant in my life—my husband, Tim—thank you *so much* for being my partner in crime and encouraging me to pursue happiness. I love you more than you know and am so blessed to live this amazing and fun life with my bestest friend ever.

Apryl Zarate Schlueter is the Chief Energy! Officer of The Cheerful Mind, Inc. *Finding Success in Balance: My Journey to The Cheerful Mind* is her first book. After years of working in various industries, such as engineering, IT consulting, teaching, and higher-education administration and finance, Apryl realized her true passion is helping overcommitted people with big dreams to have more fun while getting stuff done. Her interests are wide and varied; in her spare time, she enjoys travel, flying trapeze, stand-up comedy, and thrill-seeking activities, to name a few. Apryl lives with her husband, Tim, and two sons in Northbrook, Illinois. You can learn more about Apryl and The Cheerful Mind at www.thecheerfulmind.com and reach her via e-mail at apryl@thecheerfulmind.com.